Sussex
Steam

MICHAEL WELCH

Ra̅ils

Published by Rails Publishing

Printed by Parksons Graphics

© Michael Welch 2015
Layout by Michael Welch. Typesetting
and book production by Lucy Frontani.

Details of Michael Welch's other
railway titles can be found at
www.capitaltransport.com

Note: All of the timetable extracts used
in this book have been taken from the
Southern Region public timetable dated
15th September 1952 which was kindly
loaned by Edwin Wilmshurst.

Introduction

On 11th June 1966 Bulleid 'West Country' Class locomotive No.34012 *Launceston*
worked a special train from Blandford Forum to Brighton and took the return working
later that day. Unfortunately, the engine was in deplorable external condition and
bereft of both name and number plates and hardly made an impressive sight but, even
so, No.34012 can justly claim a place in Sussex folklore as the last steam passenger
working in ordinary BR service. After more than 125 years grimy *Launceston* had
brought down the curtain on steam traction in the county.

Strange to relate, my own love affair with steam trains in Sussex really began
before I had even set foot in the county. My family lived in Cheadle, just outside
Manchester, and were planning a move to Worthing on the south coast and as far
as I was concerned the most vital part of the preparations was the acquisition of an
'ABC' book of Southern Region (SR) locomotives – for the uninitiated this series of
regional books covered all of BR and listed every locomotive allocated to each region.
My mother purchased a copy of this indispensible little book so I would be able to
immediately identify any locomotives I saw. After I had recovered from the shock of
discovering that SR locomotive numbers began with the number '3', for reasons I
cannot logically explain the name of one particular engine captured my imagination
and it has remained one of my top favourite locomotives to this day. That engine was
Bulleid Pacific No.34045, the name of which, *Ottery St. Mary,* intrigued me but, of
course, I had no idea that it was named after a town in Devon and the name was,
therefore, quite appropriate for a 'West Country' class locomotive. Imagine my huge
joy when, against all the odds, I discovered that No.34045 just happened to be one
of five engines, out of a class of 110, that were based at Brighton shed and a 'regular'
on the inter-regional trains from Brighton along the West Coast line through
Worthing. Moreover, *Ottery St. Mary,* like all of Brighton shed's stud of Pacifics, was
kept in absolutely exemplary external condition – it always seemed to be gleaming!

The line through Worthing was, of course, almost completely monopolised by
electric multiple units but there were three star turns on weekdays, the 9.40am
Brighton to Bournemouth, 11.0am to Cardiff and the 11.30am to Plymouth, all of
which had return workings which passed through Worthing in the evening. In the
mid-1950s the Bournemouth train was sometimes worked by Brighton shed's last
remaining LBSCR Atlantic No.32424 *Beachy Head* and I have fading memories of
this immaculate engine flashing past West Worthing on the return Bournemouth to
Brighton train. The other two services were rostered for one of Brighton's stud of
five Bulleid Pacifics as far as Salisbury and Nos.34039 *Boscastle,* 34046 *Braunton,*
34047 *Callington* and 34048 *Crediton* were a regular sight on these trains, in addition
to my favourite 'Bulleid', No.34045. The drivers always seemed to sound the whistle
between West Worthing and Durrington-on-Sea stations and, despite the fact that my
home was a quarter of a mile from the line, I could catch a momentary glimpse of a
train between the trees. During the late 1950s Brighton shed gained a reputation for
poor maintenance and its Bulleid engines in particular seemed to spend long periods
out of traffic which was, perhaps, ironical because most of the class had been built
just across the tracks in Brighton works. In late 1959 the shed reportedly had no
fewer than five Pacifics and six Maunsell 'Schools' Class 4-4-0s on its books to work
four top-link duties which seems a blatant case of gross over provision! It was a sad
day when Brighton's quintet of 'Bulleids' was summoned to Eastleigh one by one for
rebuilding, never to return. Another class for which I developed considerable affection
were the elegant Billinton K Class 'Moguls' and, here again, the examples shedded
at Brighton were nearly always in clean condition. These locomotives powered goods
trains along the coast and often shunted West Worthing goods yard which was hidden
away behind the berthing shed for electric stock and could be accessed only by means

of a long headshunt. Conveniently, from my point of view, this headshunt straddled an occupation crossing and every time a shunt move was required the gleaming 'Mogul' accompanied, of course, by the rhythmic panting of its Westinghouse brake pump, would emerge from the yard and block the crossing to the considerable frustration of people wishing to cross the line – my reaction was rather different!

The year 1962 really marked the beginning of the end for steam traction in the area and will always be remembered for the virtual elimination of the old 'Brighton' classes which had been part of the railway scene in Sussex for generations. In November five K Class 'Moguls' were taken out of traffic but far worse was to come just a few weeks later. Apparently, BR's accountants had decided that the number of steam locomotives being inherited by the newly created British Railways Board needed to be considerably reduced and the result was a holocaust of steam motive power up and down Great Britain. They decreed the withdrawal of the remaining K Class engines, Maunsell 'Schools' Class 4-4-0s and the surviving LBSCR tank classes except for the ancient 'Terriers' that were still needed at Newhaven and on the Hayling Island branch. In late December 1962 redundant engines were rounded up and dumped in Hove goods yard, presenting a truly melancholy sight particularly as some of the locomotives were still in good condition and had been at work only a few hours previously. This sad development coincided with a long spell of bitterly cold weather and Brighton shed found itself desperately short of motive power with the result that, miraculously, some E4 Class engines were hurriedly rescued from the dump and returned to service. Their stay of execution was brief, however, and the last survivor in the area, No.32479, left Brighton on 1st June 1963 for breaking-up at Eastleigh. One or two 'Terriers' remained active in Sussex for use at Newhaven where weight restrictions prevented the use of heavier locomotives but closure of the West Quay Tramway in August 1963 made them redundant and the final 'Terrier' active in Sussex was reportedly No.32678. It was retained for coal stage pilot duty at Brighton and was apparently still busily employed on this work just a few hours before departing for Eastleigh on 5th October. The end came for regular steam working at Brighton in June 1964 but pockets remained in other parts of Sussex for a further year, notably on the Horsham to Guildford and Eastbourne to Tunbridge Wells lines. I was lucky enough to travel on the last BR-sponsored steam train over the 'Cuckoo Line' on 12th June 1965 while the following day I was a passenger on the Locomotive Club of Great Britain's (LCGB) 'Wealdsman' rail tour.

Writing this book has been enormously enjoyable and I hope it will give as much pleasure to readers as I have derived from its compilation. First of all, I would like to express my heartfelt gratitude to the numerous photographers who had the foresight to record the steam age in Sussex and have permitted me to borrow their cherished and irreplaceable images for publication in this album. In addition, a number of enthusiasts have kindly assisted with proof reading and suchlike and thanks are due to Chris Evans, Dave Fakes, John Langford, Graham Mallinson, and Terry Phillips. The pictures from the Kidderminster Railway Museum collection were researched by Derek Huntriss, those from the collection of the late R.C. Riley were provided by Rodney Lissenden and images held by the Bluebell Railway Museum were made available by Tony Hillman. Charles Firminger's slides were provided by Bob Bridger. Specialist information about LBSCR signal boxes was supplied by Roger Resch and the luggage labels are from the Les Dench collection.

Michael Welch
Burgess Hill
West Sussex
August 2014

Contents

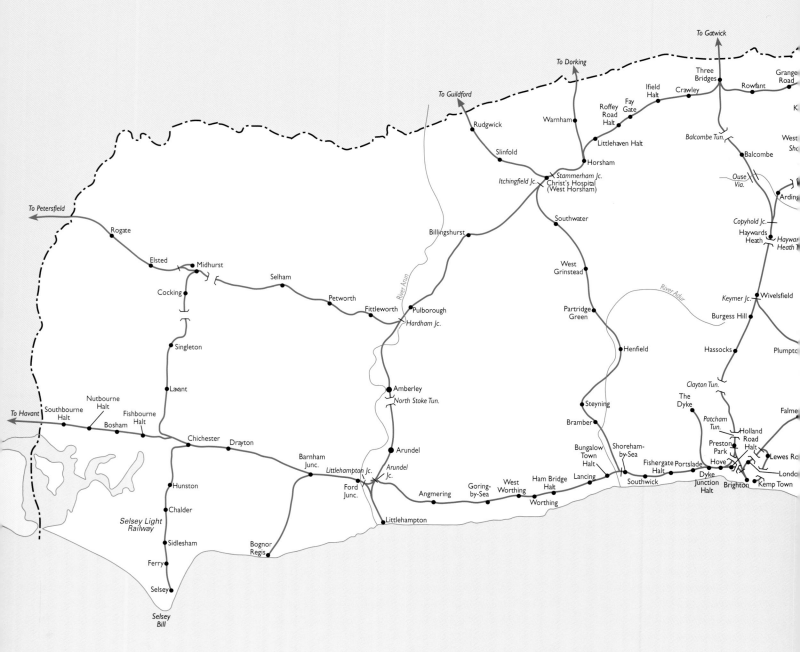

To Gatwick

Three
Bridges

Rowfant

Grange
Road

To Dorking

Ifield
Halt

Crawley

West
Sho

Roffey
Road
Halt

Fay
Gate

Balcombe Tun.

To Guildford

Warnham

Littlehaven Halt

Balcombe

Rudgwick

Slinfold

Horsham

Ouse
Via.

To Petersfield

Itchingfield Jc.

Stammerham Jc.
Christ's Hospital
(West Horsham)

Arding

Rogate

Copyhold Jc.

Southwater

Haywards
Heath

Hayward
Heath T

Elsted

Midhurst

Selham

Billingshurst

Cocking

Petworth

Fittleworth

Pulborough

West
Grinstead

Keymer Jc.

Wivelsfield

Hardham Jc.

River Adur

Burgess Hill

Singleton

Partridge
Green

Plumpto

Lavant

Amberley

North Stoke Tun.

Henfield

Hassocks

Clayton Tun.

The Dyke

Falme

To Havant

Southbourne
Halt

Nutbourne
Halt

Fishbourne
Halt

Bosham

Chichester

Drayton

Steyning

Patcham
Tun.

Bramber

Holland
Road
Halt

Arundel

Preston
Park

Barnham
Junc.

Littlehampton Jc.

Arundel
Jc.

Hunston

Ford
Junc.

Bungalow
Town
Halt

Shoreham-
by-Sea

Hove

Lewes Ro

Chalder

Angmering

Goring-
by-Sea

West
Worthing

Ham Bridge
Halt

Lancing

Fishergate
Halt

Portslade

Londo

Selsey Light
Railway

Worthing

Southwick

Dyke
Junction
Halt

Brighton

Kemp Town

Sidlesham

Littlehampton

Bognor
Regis

Ferry

Selsey

Selsey
Bill

E N G L I S H

The railway system in Sussex changed considerably during the years covered by this book as a result of line closures, so it is not possible to provide a map that would be valid for the entire period. This map shows the system as it was at its height in 1923, the year of The Grouping. It should be noted that the names of the following stations were changed at various times. The revised name is indicated in brackets. Note only major tunnels are shown.

Barnham Junction (Barnham)

Fishergate Halt (Fishersgate Halt)

Ham Bridge Halt (East Worthing Halt)

Waldron & Horeham Road (Horam)

Fay Gate (Faygate)

Dyke Junction Halt (Aldrington Halt)

Ford Junction (Ford)

Ticehurst Road (Stonegate)

To Oxted

St. Margarets Jc.

To Oxted

To Tonbridge

Tunbridge Wells Groombridge West

Tunbridge Wells Central

Strawberry Hill Tun.

Forest Row

Hartfield

Withyham

High Rocks Halt

Frant

Eridge

Wadhurst
Wadhurst Tun.

Crowborough & Jarvis Brook

Rotherfield & Mark Cross

To Tenterden

To Ashford

Sheffield Park

Mayfield

Ticehurst Road

Etchingham

Junction Road

Bodiam

Northiam

Rye

River Oure

River Rother

Robertsbridge

Tramway

Newick & Chailey

Buxted

Mountfield Tun.

Rye Harbour (Goods)

Camber

Uckfield

Heathfield

Winchelsea

arcombe

Isfield

Battle

Barcombe Mills

Waldron & Horeham Road

Cooksbridge

Crowhurst

Southerham Jc.

Warrior Square

Hastings

Ore Tunnel
Ore
Mount Pleasant Tunnel

Lewes

Glynde

Hellingly

Sidley

West St. Leonards

Hastings Tunnel

Berwick

Hailsham

West Bexhill

West Marina

Bopeep Tunnel

Central

Southease & Rodmell Halt

Normans Bay Halt

Town Newhaven

Polegate

Stone Cross Halt

Pevensey Bay Halt

Harbour

Bishopstone

Willingdon Jc.

Pevensey & Westham

Seaford

Hampden Park

Eastbourne

Beachy Head

N

0   5   10 Miles

C H A N N E L

Mention the West Coast Line to the average railway aficionado and he will immediately think of the route from London to Glasgow over Shap summit and few would suggest the Brighton to Portsmouth line. The latter route may not have the high profile of the 'Premier Line' but the Brighton to Shoreham section was the first railway in Sussex to be opened and can claim to have a station every 1¾ miles; Shoreham Airport (formerly Bungalow Town Halt) was the very first airport station in Great Britain. The origins of the West Coast line can be traced back to July 1837 when an Act of Parliament was obtained by the London & Brighton Railway (L&BR) authorising construction of the London to Brighton line plus branches to both Newhaven and Shoreham. Remarkably, the six miles-long Brighton to Shoreham branch actually opened in splendid isolation before the main London to Brighton line and the first train, which conveyed directors of the line and local tradesman, left Brighton at 3.00pm on 11th May 1840; public traffic began the following day. The opening of the Shoreham branch enabled materials needed for the construction of the main line to be shipped in through Shoreham harbour and the main route opened on 21st September 1841. It was soon realised that a westward extension from Shoreham would be desirable and powers were obtained in 1844 by the Brighton & Chichester Railway, which was nominally independent of the 'Brighton' railway, to extend along the south coast towards Chichester. The Shoreham to Worthing section opened on 24th November 1845, with the stretch on to Lyminster (near Littlehampton) opening for business on 16th March 1846. The flat terrain made construction easy and Chichester had been reached by 6th June 1846 while the section onwards to Havant was open by 15th March 1847. In the meantime the Brighton & Chichester Railway had been sold to the L&BR. There are two branches off the West Coast line that merit attention, namely those to Littlehampton and Bognor Regis. The former was originally served by a trailing junction from Ford until the present layout, which allows direct running from Brighton and Horsham, was inaugurated in 1887. The short branch from Barnham to Bognor Regis, which was originally single track, dates from June 1864; the track was doubled in 1911. The West Coast line's distinctive curving platforms are apparent in this view of LSWR M7 Class 0-4-4T No.30049 which is depicted waiting to leave Brighton with a train to Horsham on 19th August 1955. Enginemen are engaged in conversation prior to the train's departure and barrows litter the platform providing something of an obstacle course for passengers. *Mike Esau*

A Bulleid 'Light Pacific' apparently making a shunt move before reversing onto a set of coaches waiting in Platform 2 at Brighton station. This shot could have been taken at almost any time in the 1960s prior to elimination of steam on the SR but, actually, this scene was recorded during the final few weeks of steam traction at Brighton. By this time the only regular steam diagram was the 10.25am to Plymouth and its corresponding return working which were steam-hauled to and from Salisbury. There was almost no other regular steam working on the Central Division but in late 1965 the operating authorities had been forced to move the electrically-heated coaching stock (which could be diesel-worked) allocated to this service to the Oxted line where there was a desperate shortage of such vehicles. The stock used on the Plymouth service was replaced by a makeshift steam-heated rake that could be hauled (and heated, of course!) by the old Southern Railway electric locomotives, colloquially known as 'Hornbys', or steam traction. The SR was very reluctant to use steam, however, and persevered with the 'Hornbys' for a time on the section east of Havant, but changing engines at Havant or Chichester proved an operational nightmare. In addition, the steam heating boilers fitted to the 'Hornbys' proved temperamental and it was decided that it would be simpler to employ steam throughout to and from Salisbury. Here, No.34025 *Whimple* is depicted at Brighton on 12th March 1966. A special from Blandford Forum on 11th June 1966, hauled by No.34012 *Launceston* was the very last ordinary steam train from Brighton. *Charles Firminger*

The following three illustrations show everyday workings at Hove, the first station on the West Coast Line from Brighton, where the Cliftonville spur to Preston Park diverges. In this picture the 11.00am Brighton to Cardiff train, hauled by Bulleid 'West Country' Class No.34012 *Launceston,* which, as previously stated, hauled the very last BR steam train from Brighton in 1966, approaches Hove on a sunny 1st December 1962. On the left Billinton K Class 2-6-0 No.32342 waits on the London-bound spur line with the 11.07am empty stock train to Brighton which would later form the 11.30am to Plymouth. This latter train was routed via the now largely closed Exeter to Plymouth via Okehampton line which offered splendid views of desolate Dartmoor. *Charles Firminger*

In this photograph, which was taken in the early 1960s, Maunsell N Class 'Mogul' No.31830 leaves Hove goods yard with a very long goods train formed mainly of vanfits and takes the up Cliftonville spur line towards Preston Park. Note Hove 'A' signal box, which was one of two boxes that controlled movements at the station, and also the fascinating track layout. Needless to say, the latter has long since been replaced by standard track components. *Charles Firminger*

When this shot of Ivatt Class 2MT 2-6-2T No.41303 powering a Brighton-bound train was taken at Hove in late 1962 the days of the veteran M7s and H class tank engines on Horsham trains had long gone. They had been superseded in 1961 by Ivatt tank locomotives, many of which had migrated from the London Midland Region and were reportedly in poor condition, requiring main works attention before the SR would consider using them. The locomotive seen here is an exception, however, and was merely a refugee from Bricklayers Arms shed in south London; it was based at Brighton at the time of this picture. Hove marked the 'border' between the largely semaphore-signalled West Coast line and the area controlled by colour light signals operated from Brighton signal box – hence both modes of signalling are displayed on the bracket signal. *Blake Paterson*

A stay of execution. The last months of 1962 saw mass withdrawals of BR steam power in order to reduce the number of locomotives inherited by the British Railways Board and on the SR the 'Schools' Class 4-4-0s, LBSCR K Class 'Moguls' and E6 Class 0-6-2Ts were among the victims. It is thought that the withdrawal orders included the E4 Class 0-6-2Ts but at least two, Nos.32468 and 32503, stayed at work probably as a result of a dire motive power shortage caused at least in part by a prolonged spell of arctic weather. Condemned locomotives were congregated at Hove goods yard but two E4s, Nos.32474 and 32479, which had been banished to the dump, were resurrected on 12th January 1963 and returned to service. Here, No.32503 is seen shunting at Hove goods yard on 14th March 1963 with the collection of less fortunate, withdrawn engines visible in the background. On 13th April it ran light engine to Eastleigh for scrap leaving sister engine No.32479 as the sole representative of its class in the Brighton area. *Graham Mallinson*

All change at Shoreham. A lot has changed since this picture of Ivatt 2-6-2T No.41314, powering the 2.30pm Brighton to Horsham train, was taken at Shoreham-by-Sea station on 24th August 1963. The gas lighting and old 'Southern' enamel signs have been replaced while the semaphore signalling was swept away in the late 1980s. The goods yard and its associated shed have also gone while the two tall chimneys of Southwick power station, which are just visible in the background, are also things of the past. No.41314 saw service in Devon before moving to the south coast. *Charles Firminger*

Low tide at Shoreham. A fisherman digs for bait in the estuary of the river Adur as Bulleid 'Merchant Navy' Class No.35007 *Aberdeen Commonwealth* rumbles across the bridge in the afternoon sunshine with the 'Midhurst Belle' rail tour that was run to mark the complete closure of the branch to Midhurst. Attractive views of Lancing college chapel, the river Adur and the downland beyond are obtainable from trains crossing the bridge, which dates from 1911, this being a highlight of the West Coast line. Earlier the participants had been hauled by an S15 4-6-0 from Waterloo and journeyed sedately down the Guildford to Horsham line behind USA Class tank locomotive No.30064. After the run to Midhurst and back behind Q Class 0-6-0 No.30530 the train ran to Littlehampton where the 'Merchant Navy' Class engine took charge for the short hop along the coast to Brighton. There No.30530 took over the train once again and ran to Kemp Town and back before *Aberdeen Commonwealth* gave a sparkling performance over the final stage of the tour, reaching Victoria 2min early after covering the last stage from Brighton in 58min. This photograph was taken on 18th October 1964. *David Wigley*

Undoubtedly, the best-known steam locomotive ever to have run along the West Coast line from Brighton was the world famous No.4472 *Flying Scotsman*. This legendary machine was built at Doncaster works in 1923 and upon withdrawal from BR service in 1963 was purchased for preservation by Mr Alan Pegler and restored to LNER condition for main line use. On 17th September 1966 it was used on a privately sponsored special train from London Victoria to Salisbury via Brighton which is seen here passing Lancing in glorious autumn sunshine. Apart from the odd, unscheduled sortie, steam traction had been totally eliminated from Sussex by this date and crowds of enthusiasts and well-wishers lined the route along the south coast. *Flying Scotsman* was serviced at Eastleigh shed while its train was hauled to Salisbury and back by a brace of BR Standard Class 4MT 2-6-4Ts. Later in the day No.4472 returned to London by the same route so those who were unable to admire this thoroughbred in the morning were not disappointed. *Derek Penney*

BRITISH TRANSPORT COMMISSION
BRITISH RAILWAYS   B.R. 21716/478

LANCING

7 8 9 10 11 12
British Transport Commission (S)
(No.2) LANCING
PLATFORM TICKET 1d.
Available one hour on day of issue only.
Not valid in trains.   Not transferable.
To be given up when leaving platform
For conditions see over
1 2 3 4 5 6
4200   4200

A cloudless day with brilliant sunshine is not necessarily the right ingredient for a photographic masterpiece and here the wet conditions really add life to this shot of BR Standard Class 4MT No.80019 approaching Barnham in April 1964. The train is probably the Plymouth to Brighton inter-regional working for which a Bulleid Pacific would be more usual motive power, but steam traction was very much in decline in Sussex by this time so any class of engine was welcome! The tracks curving away on the left behind the signal box lead to Bognor Regis. Sadly, semaphore signalling at Barnham is no more while the attractive, brightly-coloured signal box has also gone leaving this end of the station looking rather bare. *Mike Hudson*

A platform-end scene taken at Chichester on 7th March 1959 showing LSWR M7 Class 0-4-4T No.30111 taking water while powering a Branch Line Society rail tour of local goods-only lines. This special train may not have covered long distances but, even so, there would have been plenty to interest the participants as they journeyed along the Lavant, Bishops Waltham, Droxford and Gosport branches, all of which have since been erased from the railway map. The train is stabled in a bay platform formerly used by Portsmouth to Chichester local services. The semaphore signals in the background have long since disappeared but the large signal box, which is partially visible, still survives at the time of writing. *Charles Firminger*

A view of the western approach to Chichester station which is just visible beyond the signal box in the background in this shot which was taken on 28th October 1962. Former LBSCR K Class 'Mogul' No.32345 is busy shunting the goods yard, a duty it had no doubt performed on many occasions during its long career. In steam days Chichester was the traditional motive power changeover point for goods trains coming off the South Western section and S15 Class 4-6-0s could regularly be seen turning on the triangle prior to returning home. This scene has since changed dramatically because a supermarket has sprung up on the site of the goods yard and the number of tracks has been considerably reduced. *Mike Hudson*

Beyond Chichester the West Coast line is flat and rather featureless and hardly fertile territory for railway photographers, but here is a fascinating picture taken after the Central Division had officially dispensed with steam traction following the closure of Redhill shed on 14th June 1965. This photograph shows USA Class tank locomotive No.DS235 passing Fishbourne Halt on its final journey from Lancing works to Eastleigh on 26th June 1965; presumably the photographer was 'tipped off' about this rare working. This locomotive, and its sister engine No.DS236, had been employed as works shunters at Lancing but became redundant when the carriage works there closed in May 1965. One engine was steamed for a short period each day to assist with 'clearing up' operations but when no further work could be found for them they were despatched to Eastleigh. Not long after this picture was taken No.DS235 fell victim to a 'hot box' and was observed in a siding at Fareham cooling off – the USAs had a propensity to run 'hot' on long journeys so, perhaps, it was surprising it had got that far! Sadly, both engines were cut-up at Eastleigh shed in August after BR decided, no doubt, that sending them to a south Wales scrap yard might be a trifle unwise. *The late Graham Hoare*

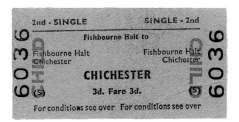

In the 1830s various schemes were put forward for a line between London and Brighton and among them was a proposal for a line through the Adur valley. In the event an independent arbitrator decided that the 'direct line' scheme (via Haywards Heath) proposed by John Rennie was the best and the plan for a line via Steyning was shelved, at least for a time. In 1857 a group of businessmen advocated a route from Dorking to Brighton via Horsham, Steyning and Shoreham and this was naturally seen as a threat to the LBSCR's buoyant Brighton traffic. The 'Brighton' company immediately came up with their own proposal for a line between Horsham and Brighton and a meeting outlining their ideas was held at the George Inn, Henfield, on 19th December 1857. It was pointed out by the LBSCR directors that the rival route would avoid Henfield and be at least a mile from Steyning and local people suspected that the LSWR was involved and only interested in gaining some of the lucrative Brighton traffic and not serving intermediate towns on the route. Both schemes survived initial scrutiny by the House of Commons but when the two plans were examined by a parliamentary committee in 1858 the LBSCR, which was anxious to serve as many Adur valley communities as possible, argued its case with such conviction it won the day and obtained an Act on 12th July 1858; the construction cost was estimated to be £155,000. Building work commenced in the spring of 1859 with the renowned Joseph Firbank as the principal contractor. Progress was steady and the first section of line, from Shoreham to Partridge Green, was brought into use on 1st July 1861, the initial service being three trains a day. There was great celebration in Steyning where church bells rang and nearly all of the local populace reportedly turned out to witness the arrival of the mid-day train from Brighton; later 70 guests assembled for dinner at the White Horse hotel in the town. The line was opened throughout as far as Itchingfield Junction, south of Horsham, on 16th September. Only a single track was laid at first but the entire line was doubled between 1877 and 1879. The river Adur is out of sight on the right of the picture as BR Standard Class 4MT 2-6-4T No.80148 accelerates past Old Shoreham with the 10.30am Brighton to Horsham train on 14th April 1962. The bridge carrying the Brighton to Portsmouth West Coast line is just visible beyond the last coach of the train, while Shoreham Airport occupies a large area on the opposite bank of the river. *Gerald Daniels*

2nd - SINGLE   SINGLE - 2nd
Horsham to
Horsham   Horsham
Shoreham-by-Sea   Shoreham-by-Sea
0391

SHOREHAM-by-SEA
via Steyning

(S)   5/3 Fare 5/3   (S)
For conditions see over For conditions see over
0391

Table 36 — **HORSHAM, SHOREHAM-BY-SEA, and BRIGHTON**

Down — Week Days

Miles	Down	a.m	a.m	a.m		a.m SX	a.m. SO	a.m SX	a.m SO		p.m	p.m SX	p.m SO	p.m	p.m SO	p.m SX	p.m SO	p.m SX	p.m SX	p.m SO	p.m	
	77 Victoria .... dep	..	5*20	6 41	..	9 18	9 18	10 18	10 18	..	12 18	1 48	2 18	3 18	4 18	4 18	5 18	5 20	6 18	5 48	7 18	..
	77 London Bridge. "	..	5 25	6[3]48	..	9[3]15	9[3]15	10Z8	10Z8	..	12H18	1[3]31	2Z8	3*16	..	4Z6	..	5 15	5 48	5[3]31	6SX48	..
	77 Waterloo...... "	..	5[3]16	6#47	..	9[3]17	9[3]7	10#17	10#17	..	12[3]17	1[3]27	2#17	2[3]27	4[3]7	4[3]17	5[3]7	5[3]7	6[3]7	5[3]27	7[3]7	..
—	**Horsham**.......... dep	..	7 16	8 12	..	10 19	10 23	11 19	11 25	..	1 39	3 19		4 19	5 19		6 19	6 25	7 19		8 19	..
2¼	Christ's Hospital K ...	..	7 21	8 16	..	10 23	10 27	11 23	11 29	..	1 43	3 23		4 23	5 23		6 23	..	7 23		8 23	..
4½	Southwater	..	7 27	8 22	..	10 29	10 33	11 29	11 35	..	1 49	3 29		4 29	5 29		6 29	6 33	7 29		8 29	..
7	West Grinstead	..	7 35	8 29	..	10 36	10 40	11 37	11 42	..	1 56	3 36		4 36	5 37		6 36	6 40	7 36		8 36	..
9¾	Partridge Green.......	..	7 41	8 36	..	10 42	10 46	11 43	11 48	..	2 2	3 43		4 43	5 43		6 43	6 46	7 43		8 42	..
11¾	Henfield..............	..	7 47	8 41	..	10 47	10 51	11 49	11 53	..	2 7	3 48		4 48	5 49		6 48	6P55	7 48		8 47	..
15½	Steyning..............	7 40	7 56	8 50	..	10 55	10 59	11 58	12 1	..	2 15	3 56		4 57	6 0		6 56	7 3	7 56		8 54	..
16	Bramber	7 42	8 0	8 54	..	10 59	11 3	12 2	12 5	..	2 18	4 0		5 1	6 3		7 0	7 6	8 0		8 57	..
20	**Shoreham-by-Sea J**..	7 51	8 10	9 5	..	11 8	11 12	12 11	12 14	..	2 28	4 9		5 11	6 13		7 9	7 15	8 9		9 6	..
21½	Southwick	7 55	..	9 9	..	..	..	..	..	..	2 32	4 13		..	6 17		7 13	..	8 13		9 10	..
23	Portslade & West Hove	7 58	8 16	9 13	..	11 14	11 18	12 17	12 19	..	..	4 17		5 17	6 21		7 17	..	8 16		9 14	..
24½	Hove..................	8 2	8 19	9 17	..	11 18	11 21	12 21	12 23	..	2 38	4 21		5 20	6 25		7 21	7 23	8 20		9 18	..
26	**Brighton** .... arr	8 7	8 24	9 22	..	11 23	11 26	12 27	12 28	..	2 43	4 26		5 25	6 30		7 26	7 28	8 25		9 25	..

Up — Week Days

Miles	Up	a.m	a.m	a.m.		p.m SX	p.m SO	p.m SO	p.m. SX		p.m.	p.m	p.m SO	p.m SX		p.m SX	p.m SO	p.m	p.m	
—	**Brighton**.......... dep	6 30	8 0	9 30	..	12 12	12 12	1 35	2 0	..	3 57	4 58	5 57	6 13	..	7 14	7 20	8 12	9 57	..
1½	Hove..................	6 34	8 4	9 34	..	12 16	12 16	1 41	2 4	..	4 1	5 2	6 1	6 18	..	7 20	7 24	8 16	10 1	..
3	Portslade & West Hove	6 38	8 8	9 38	..	..	..	1 44	2 8	..	4 5	5 6	..	6 22	..	7 23	7 28	..	10 5	..
4½	Southwick	6 42	8 12	..	..	..	..	..	..	..	4 8	5 9	..	6 26	..	..	..	..	10 9	..
6	**Shoreham-by-Sea J**..	6 46	8 16	9 44	..	12 24	12 24	1 50	2 13	..	4 12	5 13	6 9	6 29	..	7 29	7 33	8 24	10 12	..
10	Bramber	6 55	8 25	9 53	..	12 33	12 33	1 58	2 22	..	4 21	5 21	6 18	6 38	..	7 38	7 42	8 33	10 21	..
10½	Steyning..............	6 59	8 28	9 56	..	12 36	12 36	2 1	2 25	..	4 24	5 24	6 21	6 41	..	7 42	7 46	8 38	10 24	..
14½	Henfield..............	7 7	8 37	10 5	..	12 44	12 44	2 9	2 33	..	4 32	5 33	6 29	6 50	..	7 50	7 55	8 48	..	..
16½	Partridge Green.......	7 13	8 42	10 10	..	12 49	12 49	2 14	2 38	..	4 37	5 38	6 34	6 55	..	7 56	8 1	8 55	..	..
18¾	West Grinstead	7 20	8 47	10 15	..	12 55	12 55	2 19	2 4[illegible]	..	4 43	5 44	6 39	7 1	..	8 3	8 8	9 2	..	..
21½	Southwater	7 24	8 54	10 22	..	1 2	1 2	2 25	2 51	..	4 49	5 51	6 46	7 8	..	8 10	8 15	9 9	..	..
23¾	Christ's Hospital K ...	7 33	8 59	10 27	..	1 10	1 10	2 30	2 57	..	4 54	5 56	6 51	7 13	..	8 17	8 22	9 15	..	..
26	**Horsham**.......... arr	7 38	9 3	10 32	..	1 16	1 16	2 35	3 1	..	5 0	6 3	6 56	7 18	..	[illegible]	8 27	9 19	..	..
61½	77 Waterloo...... arr	9[3]4	10[3]43	12[3]3	..	2[3]42	2[3]42	4[3]13	4[3]43	..	6[3]T23	7[3]43	8[3]43	8[3]43	..	10[3]3	10[3]3	10[3]42	..	..
63¾	77 London Bridge. "	8*43	9U57	..	..	2[3]44	2[3]15	..	4 33	..	6[3]22	7[3]44	8[3]44	8[3]44	..	..	..	10[3]44	..	..
63¾	77 Victoria....... "	8 37	10 26	11 22	..	2[3]50	2 40	3 40	4[3]49	..	6[3]J33	7[3]45	8 40	8 40	..	9 40	9 40	10[3]44	..	..

Down — Sundays

Down	a.m	a.m		p.m		p.m	p.m	
77 Victoria........ dep	6 40	7 46	..	12 48	..	3 18	7 18	..
77 London Bridge "	..	7[3]55	..	12[3]30	..	2Z55	6Z55	..
77 Waterloo...... "	..	8[3]2	..	12[3]42	..	3[3]2	7[3]2	..
Horsham .... dep	8 19	9 19	..	2 40	..	4 19	8 19	..
Christ's Hospital K ..	8 23	9 23	..	2 44	..	4 23	8 23	..
Southwater	8 29	9 29	..	2 50	..	4 29	8 29	..
West Grinstead........	8 37	9 37	..	2 57	..	4 36	8 36	..
Partridge Green.......	8 43	9 43	..	3 3	..	4 42	8 43	..
Henfield..............	8 48	9 48	..	3 8	..	4z52	8 48	..
Steyning..............	8 56	9 56	..	3 16	..	5 0	8 56	..
Bramber	9 0	10 0	..	3 19	..	5 4	8 59	..
Shoreham-by-Sea J..	9 9	10 9	..	3 28	..	5 13	9 9	..
Southwick	9 13	10 13	..	..	..	..	..	..
Portslade & West Hove	9 17	10 18	..	..	..	..	..	..
Hove..................	9 20	10 22	..	3 36	..	5 21	9 18	..
Brighton.......... arr	9 25	10 27	..	3 41	..	5 26	9 23	..

Up — Sundays

Up	a.m	a.m		p.m		p.m		p.m	
Brighton.......... dep	7 23	10 8	..	2 25	..	6 25	..	8 55	..
Hove	7 28	10 12	..	2 29	..	6 29	..	8 59	..
Portslade & West Hove	7 32	10 16	..	2 33	..	6 33	..	9 3	..
Southwick.............	7 36	10 20	..	2 37	..	6 37	..	9 7	..
Shoreham-by-Sea J..	7 40	10 24	..	2 41	..	6 41	..	9 11	..
Bramber	7 49	10 33	..	2 50	..	6 50	..	9 20	..
Steyning	7 53	10 37	..	2 53	..	6 54	..	9 24	..
Henfield..............	8 1	10 45	..	3 2	..	7 2	..	9 32	..
Partridge Green	8 7	10 51	..	3 7	..	7 8	..	9 38	..
West Grinstead........	8 13	10 57	..	3 12	..	7 14	..	9 43	..
Southwater............	8 20	11 4	..	3 19	..	7 21	..	9 50	..
Christ's Hospital K....	8 25	11 10	..	3 24	..	7 27	..	9 55	..
Horsham.......... arr	8 30	11 15	..	3 28	..	7 32	..	10 0	..
77 Waterloo ...... arr	9[3]50	1[3]1	..	5[3]1	..	9[3]11	..	12[3]6	..
77 London Bridge "	9[3]57	1[3]10	..	5[3]10	..	9Z4	..	..	..
77 Victoria........ "	10 6	1 6	..	5 7	..	8 43	..	..	..

[3] Third class only
* Change at East Croydon
B Arr. 6 36 p.m on Saturdays, 1st and 3rd class
H Dep. 12 30 p.m. on Saturdays
J Station for Lancing College (2 miles)
J Arr. 6 40 p.m on Saturdays, 1st and 3rd class
K Christ's Hospital, West Horsham
P Arr. 4 minutes *earlier*
SO Saturdays only
SX or SX Saturdays excepted
T Arr. 6[3]43 a.m. on Saturdays
U Arr. 10[3]32 a.m. on Saturdays
Z Change at Sutton. Third class only between London and Sutton
z Arr. 5 minutes *earlier*

For **LOCAL TRAINS** and **intermediate Halts** between Shoreham-by-Sea & Brighton, see Table 34

For **OTHER TRAINS** between Horsham and Christ's Hospital, see Tables 34 and 38

LBSCR E4 Class 0-6-2T No.32469 accelerates away from Bramber station with a Brighton train in tow some time during the late 1950s. Most trains on the Steyning line were formed of pull-push stock at this time so it is possible that the E4 Class engine was a late substitute for a locomotive that had failed. The first two coaches in the train formed set No.652 and are of special interest, the vehicle immediately behind the engine being originally LSWR 'emigrant' third No.602 which started life in 1905 and was withdrawn in 1935. That was not the end of the story, however, because it was rebuilt with a new underframe, converted for pull-push working and renumbered 6428 before re-entering traffic. The second carriage is a former SECR ten-compartment third built by BRCW Co. in 1921 and later became Southern Railway No.1074; it was allocated to set No.652 in 1958. This set survived to become one of the last operational vintage pull-push sets on the SR, not being withdrawn until 1962. The other carriage was separate and not part of that set. *Mike Esau*

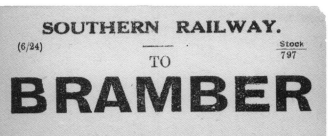

Opposite: Photographed on a dull and misty day, a Brighton to Horsham train is reflected in the still waters of the river Adur as it crosses a bridge south of Bramber in the early 1960s. The train is a pull-push working and it is being propelled by former LSWR M7 Class 0-4-4T No.30328. Pull-push working on the Steyning line was abandoned from 6th March 1961 and one immediate result of this was that SECR H Class tank locomotives disappeared from the scene but there was a marked increase in the use of LBSCR E4 Class 0-6-2T engines; however, most trains continued to be formed of pull-push stock. *Mike Esau*

On 7th October 1961 a celebration took place to mark the centenary of the Brighton to Horsham route, or the Steyning line as it was known locally. Steyning station, where an exhibition was arranged, was the focus of the festivities and the station building and signal box were specially bedecked with banners and bunting, as seen here. West Grinstead station was also decorated as part of the celebrations. In addition, BR entered into the spirit of the occasion by running two return Brighton to Horsham trips, strengthened to four coaches, hauled by LBSCR E4 0-6-2T No.32468 which was turned out in exemplary condition for the occasion and carried a small headboard. If any of the local people seen here had visited the same spot five years later they would have found a scene of utter desolation with the station closed and track lifting trains already at work on the line – just so sad. *Joe Kent / Bluebell Railway Museum*

Visitors to the Steyning line centenary celebrations crowd around LBSCR 'Terrier' 0-6-0T No.32635, the former Brighton works shunter, which was on display in the goods yard. This diminutive, colourful engine was, not surprisingly, attracting a good deal of attention and the friendly driver appears to be enjoying himself, no doubt explaining to youngsters how it all works! *Joe Kent / Bluebell Railway Museum*

The premier seaside resort on the Sussex coast is, of course, Brighton and during the summer months it attracts thousands of day trippers in addition to those taking their main holiday at the resort. With 1960s private car ownership by no means as common as it is today many people desiring a day out by the seaside took the train. Reading was a regular starting point for day excursions to Brighton but, rather than take the cross-country route via Guildford which involved reversal at Redhill – a notorious bottleneck – and a trip down the congested Brighton line, those trains were routed via Cranleigh and the Steyning line. This, of course, meant that trains had to run into Horsham and reverse there but this was infinitely better than trying to fit in yet another train on the Brighton line! In this shot the 9.22am Reading South to Brighton day excursion is seen galloping down the Steyning line with LBSCR K Class 'Mogul' No.32345 in charge on a June day in 1960. This photograph is thought to have been taken between Henfield and Steyning. *J J Smith / Bluebell Railway Museum*

Judging by the smoke being emitted from the chimney of former SECR H Class 0-4-4T No.31530 the fireman had just placed a another shovelful of coal onto its fire – perfect timing from the photographer's point of view. This photograph of a Brighton to Horsham train was taken near Partridge Green in 1960. No.31530 was constructed at Ashford works and out-shopped in July 1905; it was one of a number of these locomotives fitted with pull-push apparatus in the early years of the BR era. After a long career No.31530 was withdrawn from service in March 1962. *Mike Esau*

The 6.12pm Brighton to Horsham train, with Ivatt Class 2MT 2-6-2T No.41325 in charge, leaves West Grinstead in glorious, soft evening sunshine during the spring of 1964. Note that by this time the ancient pre-grouping carriages used on the Steyning line had given way to much more comfortable Bulleid main line sets, as seen here. The main station buildings at West Grinstead were at road level. Note rusty rails in the foreground indicating that the goods yard there was already out of use. No.41325 was originally based at Manningham (Bradford) shed and was transferred from the North Eastern to the Southern Region in September 1961. *Gerald Daniels*

There were two major sources of goods traffic on the Steyning line, Beeding cement works, between Shoreham-by-Sea and Bramber, and a brick works at Southwater which was located south of the station. The track serving the brick works can be discerned behind the goods wagons in this picture of Maunsell Q Class 0-6-0 No.30547 shunting the goods yard shortly before the withdrawal of goods facilities. The main station building, which appears to be rendered to keep out the weather, is on the right while also visible are the tiny goods shed and cattle pen. On the left the southbound platform is equipped with a waiting shelter and set of oil lamps, the signal box also being visible at the far end of the platform. It is interesting to note that there was no footbridge at Southwater and passengers who needed to cross the tracks used the boarded crossing adjacent to the signal box from where, of course, they could be observed by the signalman. This portrait of Southwater station was taken in May 1962. *Roy Hobbs*

A short northbound goods train pulls away from Southwater behind LBSCR C2X Class 0-6-0 No.32522 some time in the early 1960s. Constructed by Vulcan Foundry Ltd in August 1900 this locomotive lasted until October 1961 so it had a very good innings. Due to their origins, these machines were universally known as 'Vulcans'. *Mike Esau*

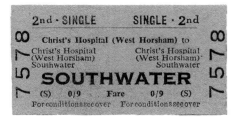

Little and large at Littlehampton! A '2-Hal' electric unit leaves Littlehampton station as Bulleid 'Merchant Navy' Pacific No.35007 *Aberdeen Commonwealth* reverses onto the stock of the 'Midhurst Belle' rail tour. This photograph was taken on 18th October 1964. The Pacific took the train as far as Preston Park from where it was shunted into Brighton station prior to a trip to Kemp Town and back. *Aberdeen Commonwealth* later gave an excellent performance during the concluding leg of the tour from Brighton to Victoria. No.35007 was probably one of the largest locomotives seen at the Sussex town while the following picture illustrates one of the smallest. *Roy Hobbs*

The long association of LBSCR 'Terrier' A1X Class locomotives with Newhaven is well known and readers could be forgiven for immediately thinking that this shot was taken there. Newhaven was not the only Sussex port where 'Terriers' shunted, however, and this portrait of No.32662 was actually taken at Littlehampton where engines of that class could be regularly seen puffing up and down the tracks along the quayside when some traffic was on offer. The presence of so many 16-ton steel mineral wagons suggests that coal was being imported there when this picture was taken in August 1961. The passenger station is located to the right and the green livery of an electric unit standing in the station can just be discerned between the two lines of wagons. *R C Riley collection*

The 3½ miles-long branch line from Barnham to Bognor Regis was opened on 1st June 1864 and electrified in the late 1930s. Following electrification, steam locomotives visiting Bognor were largely confined to goods and van trains plus the occasional seaside excursion. The very last booked steam working was a Sunday morning newspaper train from Havant which lasted until the summer of 1965. In this shot a return inter-regional excursion from Tring is seen leaving Bognor behind Stanier Class 5MT 4-6-0 No.45004 on 30th June 1957; this was apparently the first occasion one of these locomotives had visited the Sussex town. An engine shed had existed at Bognor from the earliest days of the branch but its scope was dramatically reduced following electrification in 1938 and it officially closed in 1953. Despite this, visiting engines continued to use the yard until 1958 so it presumably retained a turntable and rudimentary servicing facilities.
Edwin Wilmshurst

The Chichester to Midhurst line was, perhaps, the most lightly-trafficked of all the Sussex country branch lines, a real rural backwater if ever there was one. Construction commenced in 1865 but the Chichester & Midhurst Railway quickly ran out of funds and work came to a halt in 1868. The scheme was revived in 1876 by the LBSCR who wished to incorporate the line from Chichester with their own Pulborough to Midhurst branch and it was eventually opened by the 'Brighton' company on 11th July 1881. The line was noted for its magnificent stations which were built in a flamboyant style with generous facilities. Singleton, the station used by Goodwood race-goers, was equipped with two island platforms, both of which were presumably only really needed to cope with the crowds on a few days each year when meetings were being held. The LBSCR had its own station at Midhurst, this being situated half-a-mile east of the LSWR premises and a mile distant by road. This was not very convenient for through passengers who had to accept this situation until a new combined station was opened on 12th July 1925, from which date the LSWR premises were closed. Competition from road transport caused the Chichester to Midhurst passenger service to be withdrawn from 6th July 1935 but this event heralded what was arguably the most interesting period in the route's relatively short history. During the Second World War tunnels on the line were used for the storage of ammunition trains destined for Portsmouth while, on 19th November 1951, the line was severed when LBSCR C2X Class No.32522 fell into a stream north of Cocking after a culvert had been washed away in a storm. Goods services were withdrawn from both Singleton and Cocking from 28th August 1953 but Lavant remained open for sugar beet traffic, becoming the central loading point for this commodity over a wide area. In 1972 gravel extraction started south-west of Lavant and it was a stipulation of the planning consent that this material should be transported by rail, and this opened yet another chapter in the history of Lavant station. The line has now gone but the absolutely splendid station buildings survive as a reminder of times gone by, the only exception being Midhurst which was demolished to make way for a housing development. Country stations do not come much finer than Lavant which was photographed on 3rd August 1955; the magnificent, tall building almost dwarfs LBSCR C2X Class 0-6-0 No.32548 working a local goods train. *Edwin Wilmshurst*

During the run-down of steam traction in the 1960s rail tours became a frequent sight up and down the country and especially in the south of England where there seemed to be a trip every weekend. Operators vied with each other to devise the most interesting itineraries and very often a journey along an obscure goods-only branch line was the highlight of the day. Here, the Locomotive Club of Great Britain's 'Vectis Farewell' tour, which was run to give participants the opportunity to visit lines on the Isle of Wight threatened with closure, also included a trip on the Chichester to Lavant branch, and the special train is depicted leaving Lavant behind Bulleid Q1 Class 0-6-0 No.33020 with sister engine No.33027 assisting at the other end of the train. The participants had previously been treated to a run down the Mid Sussex line behind Bullied 'West Country' Class No.34002 *Salisbury* and, after their exertions on the island, returned to London Waterloo behind BR Standard 4-6-0 No.73155, presumably along the Portsmouth Direct line. This picture was taken on 3rd October 1965. *David Wigley*

Horsham can hardly be described as a Mecca for steam train photographers due to the dominance of electric units on the majority of services but here is a picture taken on 6th February 1955 when a rail tour visited the town, moreover this photograph is even more remarkable due to the rare motive power depicted. The train is the Railway Correspondence & Travel Society 'Hampshireman' rail tour which was run in connection with the closure to passenger trains of the Pulborough to Midhurst and Meon Valley lines. Somebody obviously thought it would be a good idea to use two of the three remaining LBSCR E5X Class 0-6-2Ts and Nos.32576 and 32570 were especially groomed for the occasion. Originally built in 1903 and 1902 respectively as E5 Class locomotives, they were rebuilt using boilers from C3 Class goods engines in 1911 but the modification did little to improve the engines' performance because, while the boiler produced a plentiful steam supply, the locomotives retained their somewhat restricted steam chests. Here, the pair of E5X engines stand at the south end of Horsham station prior to departure for Petersfield where they were relieved by a couple of T9 Class 4-4-0s; within a year both E5X Class locomotives had been withdrawn and the class rendered extinct. *J M Jarvis / Kidderminster Railway Museum*

SOUTHERN RAILWAY.
(1/44)   Stock
                    TO   787

HORSHAM

2866

British Transport Commission (S)
(No.1) HORSHAM
(S.15)
PLATFORM TICKET 2d.
Available one hour on day of issue only.
Not valid in trains. Not transferable.
To be given up when leaving platform.
For conditions see over

1 | 2 | 3 | 4 | 5 | 6

2866

Christ's Hospital station – a lost treasure. The first station down the line after leaving Horsham is Christ's Hospital which was constructed by the LBSCR in 1902 when the famous 'Bluecoat School' moved to Sussex from London. The commodious main station building was decorated by delightful stone patterns above the windows and had a very impressive frontage complete with a canopy over a small section of the approach road – in short, it was a gem. Both the main Mid Sussex line and Guildford branch platforms had a track with platforms on both sides, and Christ's Hospital was one of the few stations to have two tracks with this very unusual feature. Unfortunately, the LBSCR's high hopes that the school would generate a high volume of daily passenger business were dashed because the school's governors decreed that it would be a boarding school and the station only really came into its own at the beginning and end of each term. Even worse, in the early 1970s BR's architectural philistines ordered the demolition of the main building which was soon reduced to rubble – what an absolute tragedy. The intricately patterned waiting room window seen here gives just a hint of Christ's Hospital station's delights which are now just a memory. *Blake Paterson*

Latterly, the Guildford line platforms at Christ's Hospital station were very little used and their extremities resembled a rugby field at the neighbouring school, being covered by a luxuriant carpet of grass. At least this substantial nameboard left passengers in no doubt regarding the identity of the station. This picture was taken in the early 1960s. *J J Smith / Bluebell Railway Museum*

Most people would suggest that bright summer sunshine creates the best conditions for photography but for steam railway photography low, winter sunshine is preferable and, most importantly, the cold winter atmosphere makes escaping steam hang in the air, as seen here. This photograph of a Horsham-bound goods train, hauled by LBSCR E4 Class 0-6-2T No.32469, was taken between Billingshurst and Christ's Hospital stations in the early 1960s. The location is unremarkable but the locomotive's trail of exhaust smoke and steam really brings the scene to life. One wonders how many pictures of goods trains were taken on the Mid Sussex line. *Mike Esau*

While the year 1965 was a depressing one from the viewpoint of steam enthusiasts in Sussex, some quite surprising workings occurred often involving incursions by 'foreign' motive power and these served to enliven the scene to some degree. On 21st May the Mid Sussex line witnessed a very rare sortie by steam traction when BR Standard Class 5MT No.73021 was turned out to head a Slough to Bognor Regis excursion via Kensington (Olympia), Redhill and Horsham. No.73021 was a Western Region engine based at Gloucester, so it presumably powered the train throughout. On arrival at Bognor the Class 5MT ran along the coast to Fratton for servicing and later returned the 10-coach train to Slough. Here No.73021 is seen heading down the Mid Sussex line south of Billingshurst. *Mike Hudson*

The frontage of Pulborough station is depicted in this portrait taken on 9th May 1965. The building appears to have had neat, patterned brickwork at some stage but this has been spoilt to some degree by some new sections and, even worse, the side wall nearest the camera has been rendered to deter the worst of the weather. Pulborough station had a loop line on the London-bound side and, at one time, one or two rush-hour trains commenced their journeys there. *Stuart Ackley collection*

Hardham Junction signal box, seen here in this portrait recorded on 28th August 1966, was a delight and historically significant.
It was the last survivor of the early signal boxes on 'stilts' and dated from 1863 when the line from there to Arundel Junction was opened.
It is fairly certain that originally the corner posts would have projected beyond the roof and had signals mounted upon them.
J J Smith / Bluebell Railway Museum

Burpham signal box, between Amberley and Arundel, may not have been large but it was certainly bright and colourfully painted in the standard regional colours that were in vogue at the time; it was photographed on 18th October 1964. Burpham was a gable-ended type of box and is thought to have been built between 1910 and 1917 when it replaced Warningcamp signal box which was located a mile nearer to Arundel. Burpham was an intermediate box controlling only signals and was opened only at times of high traffic density.
J J Smith / Bluebell Railway Museum

The Locomotive Club of Great Britain's 'Sussex Coast Limited' rail tour takes the Midhurst line at Hardham Junction, south of Pulborough, on 24th June 1962; the line on the extreme right is the Mid Sussex route to Arundel. The special train is headed by two LBSCR tank engines, E4 Class No.32503 and E6 No.32417; both of these classes had been an everyday sight in the county for decades but by the time of this photograph their days were very much numbered. The E4 lasted almost another year but No.32417 was condemned at the end of 1962. Note that the Midhurst line has virtually a straight run whereas the Mid Sussex line approaches the junction on a tight curve. The Mid-Sussex Railway opened its single line from Horsham to Petworth on 10th October 1859 and most of the route was doubled when it was incorporated in the main line to Arundel Junction which opened in August 1863. Unfortunately, Petworth station was located two miles from the village it purported to serve, virtually in the middle of nowhere and almost six miles from the relatively important town of Midhurst. A new Act of Parliament was necessary to extend the branch to Midhurst and this was obtained by the Mid Sussex & Midhurst Junction Railway which soon sold out to the LBSCR. The Petworth to Midhurst line was brought into use on 15th October 1866 but it was 1872 before the intermediate station at Selham, which had been stipulated in the Act, was opened to passengers. The LSWR opened its line from Petersfield to Midhurst in 1864 after the two local companies had reached an agreement regarding their territorial claims in 1860. Closure to passengers of the Petersfield to Pulborough line occurred in 1955, the section west of Midhurst closing completely. Goods trains continued to serve Midhurst, however, until October 1964 while Petworth retained this facility until 20th May 1966. *Gerald Daniels*

Following the closure of the Pulborough to Petersfield branch to passenger traffic in 1955 a stub remained open as far as Midhurst, the rest of the line having closed completely. Goods traffic appears to have remained reasonably buoyant which is borne out here by this shot of LBSCR E4 Class 0-6-2T No.32469 rattling along with a train of sugar beet between Petworth and Fittleworth on 19th November 1960, a crisp winter's day. *Mike Esau*

BRITISH RAILWAYS (S)
PETWORTH
PLATFORM TICKET 1d
Available ONE HOUR on Day of Issue only
NOT VALID IN TRAINS. NOT TRANSFERABLE
To be given up when leaving Platform
FOR CONDITIONS SEE BACK
1 | 2 | 3 | 4 | 5 | 6

The rail tour seen in a previous illustration is portrayed again, this time passing Petworth station. Despite the seven years that have elapsed since the premises lost their passenger trains, Petworth station is still intact and the platform looked as though it was regularly swept – perhaps the station had been sold to a private purchaser. The signal box is visible on the right of the shot. One wonders when the station building had last been repainted; the paintwork certainly seems to be in very poor condition. *The late Graham Hoare*

Goods traffic, probably sugar beet, seems to have been plentiful when this portrait of Maunsell Q Class 0-6-0 No.30544 shunting at Midhurst was taken on 5th November 1960. Note the really attractive station building just visible in the background and weather-beaten station nameboard. Remarkably, both the LSWR and LBSCR had engine sheds at Midhurst in former years while another railway installation there was a quarry located south of the Petworth line. Unfortunately, the station's remoteness from the town did little to foster traffic, a situation regrettably repeated up and down the country and one that proved the undoing of many country branch lines. *Mike Esau*

Midhurst West signal box was the last survivor of two signal boxes at this location and both were designed by T. Myres Esq. to match his exquisite stations built between 1880 and 1882. Most unusually, the box was built entirely of wood to reduce the loading because it rested on specially created earthworks. Hopefully, the specification allowed for the extra weight of the visiting enthusiasts! The precise date of this picture is unknown but it is thought to have been taken in February 1955 when a rail tour visited Midhurst. The structure is in very shabby condition and was clearly long overdue for a repaint. *R C Riley collection*

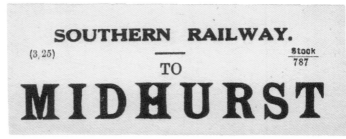

SOUTHERN RAILWAY.

(3, 25)

TO

Stock 787

MIDHURST

The Horsham to Guildford branch line – a true backwater. The Sussex county border was located between Rudgwick and Baynards stations so only the southern section of this line qualifies for inclusion in this album. Fanciful though it may seem, the promoters of the Horsham & Guildford Direct Railway Company originally envisaged the line as part of a through route from the Midlands to the south coast and they needed to retain the goodwill of both the LSWR and the LBSCR. Unfortunately, in the late 1850s those two companies were at loggerheads and at first neither supported the construction of a Horsham to Guildford line. On 6th August 1860, however, an Act was passed authorising the route and this gave vital running rights into Guildford station. Later the line's original proposers faded from the scene and it was left to the 'Brighton' company to negotiate directly with the hostile LSWR. Construction eventually began in 1862 and the line was opened for traffic on 2nd October 1865. The route was destined to have a very quiet existence,

however, because the LBSCR enjoyed cordial relations with the London & North Western Railway whose through trains from the Midlands and north of England could be routed down the West Coast main line to Kensington and on to the south coast, rather than via Guildford. In the 1890s it is recorded that seven trains a day operated along the branch, a figure that remained fairly constant throughout the life of the line. When main line services to Guildford and Horsham were electrified in the late 1930s the branch that connected the two towns was left as an outpost of steam traction and the outbreak of the Second World War put paid to any possibility of it being electrified. Strangely, the line's origins as a LBSCR branch meant that the officially recognised direction of travel to London was via Horsham and connections at Guildford were not widely advertised. The 1950s saw a steady decline in the line's goods traffic and the final booked goods working ran on 4th September 1962. On the passenger side M7 Class 0-4-4Ts, working motor trains, were very common for many years with E4 Class 0-6-2Ts from Horsham shed also appearing on a regular basis. Latterly, Ivatt-designed Class 2MT 2-6-2Ts, some of which had been drafted in from other regions, monopolised services. Towards the end Guildford shed was not averse to turning out a Bulleid Q1 Class 0-6-0 for a Horsham branch passenger turn and the three-coach trains must have been a plaything for these powerful machines. Here, No.33006 poses in Horsham station after arriving with the 6.05pm from Guildford on 27th April 1964. *Graham Mallinson*

Table 38 — GUILDFORD and HORSHAM *(timetable, detail illegible)*

Slinfold station was equipped with standard BR 'sausage' signs in SR colours and these were mostly fixed to the ornate platform lamps, as seen here. This picture was taken shortly before closure on 28th May 1965. *R C Riley*

The station at Slinfold was the first on the branch from Horsham and as pretty a country station as one would wish to see. The single-platform station can be seen beyond the level crossing with an Ivatt 2-6-2T coming to rest with a train from Guildford. The large building was the stationmaster's house and facilities for passengers were probably modest. Note the wooden level crossing gate and a sternly worded notice advising that 'the wicket gates are not controlled by the company in any way' and persons using them should 'stop, look and listen for approaching trains'. The milepost is of particular interest because it indicates the mileage from London Bridge via East Croydon and not Waterloo, thus emphasising the route's LBSCR origins. This portrait was taken on 12th June 1965, the last day of normal services. *The late Graham Hoare*

Most of the Horsham to Guildford line ran in Surrey and is, therefore, outside the scope of this album, the last station in Sussex being Rudgwick which is depicted in this early 1960s view. The goods yard is being lifted following the end of goods traffic but the station itself remains intact apart from the removal of signal arms. Rudgwick station has one particular claim to fame because it was the last in the area to boast a wagon turntable which was a familiar sight in goods yards in times gone by. Wagons were moved by horse or manpower, very often aided by a pinch bar levered between the rail and one wheel. Note the brilliant autumn colours in this shot which was taken looking northwards. *Gerald Daniels*

The activities of photographers on the right and a small gathering of onlookers on the platform at Rudgwick give an immediate clue to the date of this picture. Yes, it was taken on the last day of regular passenger services which was Saturday 12th June 1965. Note also the large number of people hanging out of the carriage windows of this train from Horsham hauled by a bunker-first Ivatt tank locomotive. The station building seems to be well-maintained and the rest of the station is in quite tidy condition, apart from encroaching weeds. The following day a rail tour hauled by a brace of specially cleaned Q1 Class engines from Guildford shed traversed the line and that, as they say, was that. *The late Graham Hoare*

Various proposals for a line linking London and Brighton were put forward in the early 1830s and in 1835 no fewer than six schemes were considered by Parliament. They could be broadly classified as the 'direct' schemes that went straight across the grain of the Weald or the routes via the river Adur gap that were less direct but cheaper to construct. Eventually, Parliament ruled in favour of John Rennie's direct line and an Act was passed on 15th July 1837 authorising the London & Brighton Railway to construct a line from a junction with the London & Croydon Railway 'at or near Selhurst farm' (south of Norwood Junction) to Brighton. In addition, branches were also approved from Brighton to Shoreham and Newhaven, the total authorised capital being £180,000. The engineer was John Urpeth Rastrick and by 1840 6,206 men and 960 horses were said to be at work on the construction and the population of small villages such as Balcombe was swelled considerably by this workforce. Materials could be shipped into Shoreham harbour and the section of line between Brighton and Shoreham was, therefore, given priority; this opened on 12th May 1840. Substantial progress was being made on the line's engineering works and the Ouse viaduct was ready by March 1841 while Balcombe tunnel had also been completed. On 28th June 1841 an inspection of the route as far as Haywards Heath was carried out and on 12th July passenger services between London Bridge (Victoria did not open until 1860) and Haywards Heath commenced, four weekday trains in each direction being provided. A ceremonial opening of the final stretch down to Brighton took place on 21st September with public services commencing on the same day. The Brighton line was boldly planned and excellently laid out, striking across the grain of the Weald upon a switchback profile with three gable summits. The earthworks were heavy, but the ruling gradient of 1 in 264 and absence of curves enabled trains to run at a relatively high speed once Croydon had been passed, the only limiting factor in later years being the density of traffic. Major landmarks in the later history of the Brighton line are the formation of the LBSCR in July 1846, the opening of the Quarry line (avoiding a bottleneck at Redhill) which came into use for passenger services in April 1900 and the quadrupling which was completed in stages as far as Balcombe Tunnel Junction by 1912. It could be argued, however, that the most momentous day in the line's history was New Year's Day 1933 when full electric services were introduced. This picture was taken at Brighton station on 13th April 1958 and depicts Maunsell 'King Arthur' Class 4-6-0 No.30796 *Sir Dodinas le Savage* waiting to depart for Victoria with the 'Brighton Atlantic Farewell' rail tour. The participants were no doubt looking forward to a fast run up to Victoria, this being a rare treat for steam enthusiasts on the Brighton line which was normally the preserve of electric traction. The thoughts of most participants, however, were probably dominated by the fact that earlier in the day they had travelled down from London to Newhaven hauled by LBSCR H2 Class 'Atlantic' No.32424 *Beachy Head,* the last survivor of a legendary class that was making its last public run prior to withdrawal. *R C Riley*

A portrait of Brighton station, taken on 9th February 1962, showing Bulleid 'Battle of Britain' Pacific No.34055 *Fighter Pilot* making a dramatic, smoky exit from Platform 7 with the 1.55pm to Victoria via Uckfield. This shot was taken from the footbridge to the former signal box that spanned the tracks and provided a panoramic view of the station and the quite complex track layout. Sadly, 1962 proved to be No.34055's last full year in traffic because, in June 1963, it became one of the first Bulleid Pacifics to be taken out of service, Nos.34035/43/74 being the other casualties during that month. The west wall of the former Brighton locomotive works is on the left of the picture. *Edwin Wilmshurst*

It may, at first sight, seem highly unlikely but LBSCR 'Terrier' 0-6-0T No.DS377 and its load of Isetta bubble cars had at least one thing in common – they were both products of Brighton works. Following the closure of the works for railway purposes in the mid-1950s, Brighton works was leased to Isetta for the assembly of these rather strange looking vehicles that were in fashion at the time. The works sidings were still shunted using ancient steam traction and trainloads of these brightly coloured cars could often be seen being shunted around the station area by 'Terrier' tank engines that were from an entirely different age. This intriguing picture was taken in the Top yard at Brighton on 30th May 1958. One wonders whether Isetta's specification included a Brighton works maker's plate and, if so, where was it affixed to the vehicle? *J H W Kent / Bluebell Railway Museum*

The photographer appears to have discovered the best railway photographic location in Brighton and certainly one previously unknown to the author. This wonderfully panoramic photograph depicts the 12.27pm Brighton to Leicester train passing the Top yard and tracks serving Lovers Walk electric depot behind LBSCR 'Atlantic' No.32426 *St. Alban's Head* on 12th July 1952. London Road viaduct, which is partially visible, and the rooftops of Brighton form the backdrop while the cluster of buildings on top of the hill in the far background is that of Brighton General Hospital. In the summer 1957 timetable this train was routed along the now closed route from Northampton (Castle) to Market Harborough and was booked to reach Leicester (London Road) at 4.06pm so it was quite an interesting run.
J J Smith / Bluebell Railway Museum

BRITISH RAILWAYS (S)
One Perambulator or Child's Mail Cart
accompanying Passenger at Owner's risk
(No.2) Brighton to (No.2)
ANY STATION
NOT EXCEEDING
5 MILES DISTANT
Rate 6d. A
FOR CONDITIONS SEE BACK

Portrait of a faded star. A very run-down looking Maunsell 'Schools' Class 4-4-0, No.30915 *Brighton,* takes the 7.15pm Brighton to Oxford return excursion past Waterhall, just north of Patcham tunnel, on 10th June 1962. This was once a relatively peaceful spot but this location has since been changed out of all recognition following the construction of the Brighton by-pass and its associated link roads. No.30915, which was once burnished to perfection for hauling the Royal train, spent most of 1962 based at Redhill shed but was working from Brighton depot at the end of the year, one of its last duties being a Brighton to Salisbury turn. *Brighton* survived until the end of that year, being withdrawn when the entire 'Schools' class was eliminated in December 1962. *Joe Kent / Bluebell Railway Museum*

The delightful Billinton K Class 'Moguls' were one of the author's all-time favourite locomotive types, No.32353 being depicted here, but it has to be admitted that it is the castellated portal of the northern end of Clayton tunnel that really catches the eye in this picture. It is one of the best-known landmarks on the Brighton line but rail passengers obtain only a brief glimpse as their train speeds past. The justification for this impressive portal is not entirely clear but it is said that in the early days of train travel passengers were frightened of dark and smoky tunnels and the portal's castellation represented strength and security which reassured those of a nervous disposition. However, the southern entrance to Clayton tunnel, which was not embellished in any way, offered no such reassurance. The train is the Locomotive Club of Great Britain's 'Sussex Coast Limited' rail tour and this shot was taken on 24th June 1962. *The late Graham Hoare*

A Walsall to Hastings holiday train, in charge of Maunsell 'Schools' 4-4-0 No.30901 *Winchester,* passes Burgess Hill station on 29th July 1961. After coasting down from Balcombe tunnel, almost nine miles distant, the crew would doubtless have been aware that the next four miles were uphill, mainly on a gradient of 1 in 264, as far as the southern entrance to Clayton tunnel, whence it was downhill all the way to Brighton. The location of Burgess Hill station, at the southern end of a deep cutting, provides an interesting background, making it a worthwhile spot for photographers, but few pictures seem to have been taken there in steam days. Note the gas station lighting and Southern Railway enamel sign. *Joe Kent / Bluebell Railway Museum*

On 5th October 1952 the Railway Correspondence & Travel Society marked the centenary of Brighton works by organising a Pullman special from Victoria to Brighton and return using Brighton 'Atlantic' No.32424 *Beachy Head;* the train was presumably over-subscribed because a fortnight later a repeat tour ran using sister engine No.32425 *Trevose Head.* In each case the train comprised eight sumptuous Pullman carriages, a real treat for the participants after years of post war austerity. During the layover at Brighton passengers were kept 'entertained' by a shuttle service that ran to Kemp Town and back. In this picture, which is the earliest colour action shot taken in Sussex ever seen by the author, No.32424 is depicted approaching Haywards Heath in glorious autumn sunshine on the return trip to London; the lofty Rocky Lane bridge provides an interesting background. What a wonderful day out employing classic LBSCR motive power. *J M Jarvis / Kidderminster Railway Museum*

Motive power from other regions was a regular sight on the Brighton line for many years, especially Stanier Class 5MT locomotives on post-war excursions from the Midlands to the south coast resorts on summer weekends. During the Second World War there were diagrammed workings between Willesden and Three Bridges yard which brought a variety of types to Sussex. An exceptional working occurred on 4th June 1965 when former LMSR 8F Class 2-8-0 No.48544, of Bletchley shed, powered a mammoth Newcastle to Hove train of 20 pigeon vans plus a support coach, which is seen here getting away from Haywards Heath after taking water. The 8F retired to Redhill shed from where it was reportedly used on local workings before returning northwards with the empty pigeon vans on 8th June. Three days later a 'Black Five' worked to Crawley on a similar train. Brighton line commuters have campaigned for years for longer trains to ease chronic overcrowding in the rush hours so they must have envied the 20 vehicles that BR obligingly turned out for the, no doubt, very appreciative pigeons! *David Clark*

A false impression? On 17th August 1963 Bulleid Q1 Class 0-6-0 No.33015 took over the 10.20am SO Hastings to Sheffield Victoria through train at Brighton and appears to be well in control as it passed Haywards Heath. Unfortunately, No. 33015 got no further than Three Bridges where it was declared a failure apparently due to shortage of steam and N Class 'Mogul' No.31401 was provided as a replacement. At least the incident would have given the holiday-makers something to talk about during the long journey home after their holiday.
Graham Mallinson

On 23rd June 1960 a party special from Newmarket was worked throughout to Brighton by B1 Class 4-6-0 No.61287 of Cambridge shed. The photographer recorded that it was booked to commence its return journey at 6.57pm and the B1 is seen simmering in Platform 7 at Brighton station while a six-car electric unit stands at an adjacent platform. B1s were hardly regular visitors to the south coast but in fact No.61287 was not the only member of its class to venture to Brighton during 1960 because, on 8th August, No.61137 powered a special from Leicester Central and carried a huge circular headboard lettered 'City of Leicester Central Holiday Express'.
J J Smith / Bluebell Railway Museum

When No.9017, the last GWR 'Dukedog', was withdrawn from traffic in October 1960 a fund was set up to preserve the locomotive and while money was being raised BR obligingly put the engine into store at the former Cambrian Railways' locomotive works at Oswestry. In early 1962 No.9017 was purchased and its future secured, but there remained the problem of finding a suitable home for the locomotive because at that time standard gauge railway preservation was in its infancy and there were few sites available. Following negotiations between the various parties it was agreed that the 'Dukedog' would be moved to the Bluebell Railway and No.9017 journeyed southwards in February 1962. The locomotive doubtless travelled down from Shropshire chimney first, but the Bluebell authorities wanted it facing northwards so a special trip down to Brighton was arranged purely for turning purposes. Here, No.9017 is depicted reversing towards Brighton shed on 15th February 1962, the first, and no doubt the last, time one of these distinctive engines will visit the south coast. *Edwin Wilmshurst*

A very lucky locomotive. A shot taken at Brighton shed on 12th September 1963 showing USA Class tank locomotive No.DS238 *Wainwright* undergoing major surgery. This machine was originally built by Vulcan Ironworks, Pennsylvania, USA, in 1943 for the war effort but it is doubtful whether it ever turned a wheel in war service and by 1947 found itself stored at Newbury racecourse, together with other engines of the same class, as war surplus material. The Southern Railway snapped up 14 USA Class locomotives at a bargain price for use in Southampton docks where, following overhaul and modification to suit British standards, they worked until replaced by diesel shunters in the early 1960s. This particular example was formerly No.30070 and in 1963, at a time when other engines in the class were being scrapped, No.30070 was lucky enough to be granted a new lease of life as a works shunter at Ashford. It was given a thorough overhaul at Eastleigh works in July 1963 and repainted in light green livery as seen here. Regrettably, the USAs were prone to 'run hot' on long journeys for which they were not really designed, and No.DS238 was suffering from a hot box when it arrived at Brighton on 8th September. It resumed its journey eastwards on 6th October but developed another hot axle box and had to be sidelined at Appledore, where it was observed exuding 'acrid smoke'. Later in its career No.DS238 had further good fortune when it 'ran hot' yet again when *en route* from Ashford to south Wales for breaking-up in late 1967. BR promptly washed its hands of the problem by selling No.DS238, and its Ashford works companion No.DS237 *Maunsell,* to the Kent & East Sussex Railway at Tenterden, where they survive today. So, hot boxes, the achilles heel of the class, at least ensured the salvation of two of them. Two lucky locomotives! *David Wigley*

Facing page lower: The romance of the steam age? Many people look back on the steam era with affection but for those involved with the day to day maintenance of the steam fleet the work was usually arduous, dirty and sometimes downright dangerous. Note the piles of hot ash and the unguarded pit in this picture taken at Brighton shed on 23rd June 1956. The locomotive is N15X Class 4-6-0 No.32329 *Stephenson,* a member of a class that was rarely photographed in colour because it became extinct before colour photography became commonplace. *Stephenson* had just been turned after arriving in Brighton with, appropriately, a Stephenson Locomotive Society rail tour. It was originally built at Brighton works, to Billinton's design, as an L Class 4-6-4T and was released from the works in October 1921 for express passenger work on the Brighton and Eastbourne lines; the unusual wheel arrangement was not found on any other system south of the river Thames. When those routes were electrified in the 1930s the engines were redundant and rebuilt by Maunsell in 1934-36 as 4-6-0 tender locomotives with eight-wheel tenders. They were transferred to the Western Section and worked initially from Nine Elms shed and five engines were loaned to the GWR during the Second World War. After the war the locomotives returned and were based at Basingstoke for secondary duties but they comprised a small, non-standard class and withdrawals commenced in 1955. *Stephenson* was withdrawn from service two months after this shot was taken while the final survivor lasted until July 1957. Note the Fairburn Class 4MT 2-6-4T locomotive on the left of the picture. *W Potter / Kidderminster Railway Museum*

Below: The gloomy interior of Brighton shed was typical of many steam locomotive sheds up and down the country and some were in much worse condition than Brighton which had benefited from considerable investment in the late 1930s when a new roof was provided. In this illustration a selection of motive power can be seen, including a K Class 'Mogul' on the left and a pair of 'Brighton' tank engines on the right. Outside in the sunshine are a BR Standard 2-6-4T and 'Schools' Class 4-4-0 while (what appears to be) a Maunsell 'Mogul' is receiving attention under the hoist. This picture was taken in late 1962 just prior to the *en masse* withdrawal of many of the older classes. *Blake Paterson*

The last days of Brighton shed. This picture of BR Standard Class 4MT No.80017 standing under the hoist was taken on 18th April 1964, two months before the shed was closed. The almost empty shed yard tells its own story and the only engines visible, apart from No.80017 and a diesel, are three Ivatt 2-6-2Ts which were still in charge of the Brighton to Horsham trains, until they were replaced by diesel units from 4th May. The only regular steam turn that remained after that date involved working the Lancing workmen's train, known locally as the 'Lancing Belle', and even this was a pale shadow of its former self. In the past this heavy train, which conveyed workmen to and from Lancing works, had always been double-headed, but the works had been earmarked for closure and many staff had already left so the train had been slimmed down to only six coaches and one locomotive. The 'Belle' remained steam worked until 15th June from which date Brighton shed closed and the curtain came down on 120 years of steam railway history in the town. The young train spotter visible on the right had left it a bit late! *W Potter / Kidderminster Railway Museum*

BRIGHTON MOTIVE POWER DEPOT

Between 1841 and 1876 the population of Brighton trebled, encouraged by the coming of the railway and the resort's increasing popularity among the masses. The LBSCR had a monopoly of the lucrative railway traffic and other companies wished to grab a share, and in 1863 a Beckenham, Lewes & Brighton Railway was proposed, this being sponsored by the LBSCR's rivals, the 'Chatham' and 'South Eastern' companies. The LBSCR was alarmed by this scheme and other associated plans, so it built a number of routes in east Sussex in order to forestall its rivals. The LBSCR's Kemp Town branch was one such line that was constructed to deter other railway companies who planned to invade its territory in addition to providing a local train service for the rapidly developing eastern part of Brighton. It was, however, an extremely costly line to construct due to a 1,024 yards-long tunnel and two viaducts, one of fourteen arches and another of three arches. The 1¼ miles-long line diverged from the Brighton to Eastbourne route at Kemp Town Junction, situated just beyond Ditchling Road tunnel; it was opened on 2nd August 1869. There were two intermediate stations, Lewes Road, and Hartington Road, but the latter was only open from January 1906 to April 1911, so it was very short lived. Unfortunately, the Kemp Town branch was a very circuitous route and vulnerable to competition from a direct and frequent tram service and passenger services were withdrawn from 1st January 1933. Goods traffic was buoyant, however, and the branch survived for almost another 40 years serving the old Kemp Town station which was officially known as 'Brighton East Goods Depot'. Needless to say, the novelty of a trip along the branch proved irresistible to many enthusiasts and in this picture the Brighton works shunter, A1X Class 0-6-0T No.DS377, poses at Kemp Town with two pristine 'Brighton' coaches on 23rd June 1956. Could BR have provided a more colourful train? *W Potter / Kidderminster Railway Museum*

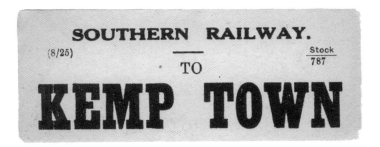

The visit of the preserved Caledonian Railway 'Single' locomotive No.123 was undoubtedly the highlight of 1963 for enthusiasts in Sussex, its blue livery and elegant design attracting many favourable comments from admirers. Built by Neilson & Co. of Glasgow in 1886, the locomotive took part in the famous 'races to the north' in 1888 and was eventually withdrawn from ordinary traffic in 1935. In 1958 the Scottish Region made the inspired decision to restore No.123 to full working order for use on special trains north of the border and it is most unlikely they contemplated that the 'Single' would ever work south of the border, let alone travel as far south as Sussex! But that is exactly what happened on 15th September 1963 when, accompanied by preserved LSWR T9 Class 4-4-0 No.120, it powered the Bluebell Railway's 'Scottish Belle' rail tour from Victoria to Haywards Heath and return. The pair ran down to Brighton shed for servicing and are seen here after being turned in readiness for their journey to Horsted Keynes where they were positioned for photographic purposes during the afternoon prior to their run back to London. Note the 'white' coal in the tender of No.123, that being an old LBSCR tradition. The white-painted arch on the front of the shed building is of particular interest because it was left *in situ* when the shed was rebuilt in the late 1930s and is a reminder of how the entire front of the shed would have looked prior to the rebuilding. *W Potter / Kidderminster Railway Museum*

After being on display at Horsted Keynes the two veterans returned to Haywards Heath and are depicted setting off for Victoria in the autumn afternoon sunshine; the rooftops of a leafy residential area of the town provide the backdrop. The locomotives are crossing over from the down loop platform to the up fast line, a manoeuvre that cannot be made at this location today following track alterations made during the re-signalling of the Brighton main line. The coach in the shot is one of twenty general saloons intended for boat train traffic and constructed in 1933; they were universally known as 'Nondescript Brakes'. These carriages masqueraded as first class vehicles for race traffic, second class on boat trains and third class for schools parties or excursions, so they were nothing if not flexible. The seating was quite luxurious with seats akin to armchairs which had separate armrests, so every passenger had plenty of room – those were the days! *W Potter collection / Kidderminster Railway Museum*

2nd SPECIAL EXCURS.ON
The Bluebell Railway
Preservation Society.
"SCOTTISH BELLE"
(C.M.9952) 22nd. SEPT.1963
Victoria or East Croydon to
SHEFFIELD PARK
Via Haywards Heath & Horsted Keynes
AND RETURN
(S)   (S)
FOR CONDITIONS SEE OVER
0218   0218

THE CALEDONIAN RAILWAY 'SINGLE' VISITS SUSSEX

The Bluebell Railway enjoyed very cordial relations with the owner of Great Northern Railway (GNR) 0-6-0 saddle tank locomotive No.1247, the very first engine bought for private operational preservation, and it was arranged that the locomotive would work a rail tour to the Bluebell on 1st April 1962. There was only a small number of preserved locomotives in working order in the early 1960s so the visit of No.1247 was a special treat for Bluebell members; the train used the Ardingly connection to Horsted Keynes which was still in use at that time. The tour started from London Bridge station, No.1247 having enjoyed overnight hospitality at Bricklayers Arms shed after travelling down from its base at Hatfield the previous evening. Here, No.1247 is seen steaming along the quadruple track section north of Balcombe tunnel with its six-coach train in tow. On arrival at Haywards Heath the train reversed prior to running to Horsted Keynes where *Stepney* coupled on to the rear for the short journey to Sheffield Park. *Gerald Daniels*

The 'Blue Belle' rail tour later returned from Sheffield Park to Horsted Keynes with many onlookers lining the route despite the fact that the engine they had come to see was on the south end of the train! On arrival at Horsted Keynes the special reversed yet again and is depicted here heading along the Ardingly branch *en route* to Haywards Heath where yet another reversal took place. *The late Graham Hoare*

GNR No.1247 HAULS A RAIL TOUR TO THE BLUEBELL RAILWAY

One of the best photographic locations in Sussex is, without a doubt, just north of the Ouse viaduct, between Haywards Heath and Balcombe, and this magnificent structure looks its best in soft afternoon sunshine, as seen here. This Victorian masterpiece of civil engineering consists of 37 arches and is 1,475ft long; 11 million bricks were reputedly used in its construction, some of which were brought up the river Ouse in barges. No.1247 is working hard up the 1 in 264 gradient that applies almost as far as the former Balcombe Tunnel signal box. On the return journey the veteran reportedly performed brilliantly and was routed via the Quarry line while the 'Brighton Belle' was relegated to the slower route via Redhill. What a memorable day it must have been! *Charles Firminger*

GNR No.1247 HAULS A RAIL TOUR TO THE BLUEBELL RAILWAY

Three Bridges to Tunbridge Wells West – a delightful Sussex byway. This line was opened in two distinct sections, the first being on 9th July 1855 when the single track branch line from Three Bridges to East Grinstead opened for traffic. There was a wait of eleven years before the line through to Tunbridge Wells was completed by the East Grinstead, Groombridge & Tunbridge Wells Railway, this opening on 1st October 1866. Regrettably, this lovely little line was closed from 2nd January 1967, a surprising and short-sighted decision in view of the route's close proximity to London. Branch trains used the bay platform at Three Bridges and here M7 Class 0-4-4T No.30053 is seen ready to leave with the 4.08pm train to East Grinstead on 14th March 1963. Since this shot was taken the buildings on the down main line platform have completely disappeared and at the time of writing the site is partly occupied by the Three Bridges area signalling centre. *Graham Mallinson*

Down in the woods something puffed...the contrast between the Three Bridges to Tunbridge Wells route and the nearby and exceptionally busy, quadruple track Brighton line could not have been greater. Here, M7 Class 0-4-4T No.30133 puffs gently along between the trees with an eastbound train on a sunny 30th March 1963. There was never any desperate urgency on the Three Bridges to Tunbridge Wells route – it simply wasn't that kind of line. *Roy Hobbs*

Rowfant station was situated in a quiet rural setting and this, together with the distinctive buildings, acted as a magnet for railway photographers: more pictures of Rowfant were submitted for this book than any other station of a similar status. Another factor in the plentiful supply of pictures taken at Rowfant is the fact that pre-grouping steam locomotives could be seen at work on the line until early 1964, quite late in the day for the Central Section. The station began life in 1855 and, although it was open to the general public, it was really provided for the local landowner, Curtis Miranda Lampson, in recognition of his generosity in sacrificing a strip of land to enable the railway to pass. Hopefully, the following selection of illustrations give at least some idea of everyday 'comings and goings' at this little station during the closing years of the steam era. An item of exceptional interest at Rowfant was the most unusual, hand operated level crossing which was needed because the lane crossed the railway at a very acute angle. Note the alcove on the end of the station building which, according to local folklore, was provided as a refuge for the landowner's coachman. This picture was taken looking towards East Grinstead in November 1961. *Stuart Ackley collection*

Rowfant – the quintessential English country station? Photographed in beautiful autumn sunshine former SECR H Class 0-4-4T No.31544 pauses with an East Grinstead-bound pull-push train on 29th September 1962. Note the station building's decorative chimneys and barge boards, not to mention the elegant oil lamp. One wonders, however, whether the landowner for whom it was built was a regular passenger!
The late Graham Hoare

A shot taken at Rowfant during the dreadfully harsh winter of 1962/63, showing BR Standard Class 4MT 2-6-4T No.80087 making a brisk departure towards East Grinstead with a two-coach train. Note the deep snow on the platform; it must have been bitterly cold but, even so, a hardy (foolhardy?) passenger has deigned to stick his head out of the window. Full marks to the photographer for taking this perfect Christmas card scene – his fingers must have been rather numb! *Roy Hobbs*

But it didn't always snow at Rowfant! Four months after the previous shot was taken spring had definitely arrived, the sun was shining and the trees were already in leaf as evidenced here by this portrait of H Class 0-4-4T No.31518 waiting to leave with a pull-push train for Three Bridges on 27th April 1963. The coaches are Maunsell-designed vehicles originally built in the 1930s for main line use and converted by BR between 1959 and 1961 for pull-push operation on branch lines, where they replaced much older carriages. *David Clark*

In the late 1950s there were 46 vintage pull-push sets, similar to the type seen here, operating on the SR and doubts were expressed about their safety, particularly their crash-worthiness and likelihood of them catching fire if involved in an accident in the third rail area. In addition, in 1959 the British Transport Commission decreed that any carriage more than 30 years old should be withdrawn and this brought matters to a head. Some 'new' sets were introduced, comprising suitably modified Maunsell coaches, and these replaced the veteran, pre-grouping pull-push sets which were consigned to the scrap heap. Set No.723, seen here being propelled into Rowfant station when forming the 4.27pm East Grinstead to Three Bridges train on 18th September 1960, was built by the LBSCR in about 1922. The driver can be clearly seen sitting comfortably in the cab while his fireman was doing his best to produce plenty of steam on the locomotive, in this case M7 Class 0-4-4T No.30055. *Gerald Daniels*

A train for East Grinstead makes a quick exit from Grange Road station in early 1963 behind M7 Class 0-4-4T No.30053. This locomotive was destined to become internationally famous, and the most widely travelled M7 Class engine, when it was shipped to the Steamtown Railway Museum in Vermont, U.S.A. in 1967. Twenty years later it was rescued by the Southern Repatriation Group who returned it to its old haunts at the Swanage Railway in Dorset. *Blake Paterson*

The author was really delighted when this picture of a LMSR-designed Fairburn tank engine was submitted for inclusion in this album – it was the only colour shot of one of these locomotives offered for publication. A batch of 41 of these very competent machines was built at Brighton works in the early 1950s and 34 remained on the SR until early 1960, working on the Central and South Eastern sections. On the Central Section they replaced a motley collection of pre-grouping engines that was completely worn out after years of wartime neglect. The Fairburn locomotives were largely based at Brighton, Stewarts Lane, Three Bridges and Tunbridge Wells West sheds and used principally on the Oxted line, where the stiff gradients and heavy commuter trains dictated the use of powerful engines. In this picture No.42091 is seen pausing at East Grinstead (High Level) in the course of working a Victoria to Tunbridge Wells West train in February 1958. These locomotives were an integral part of the railway scene in Sussex for a decade but their role seems to have gone largely unrecorded in colour, though a fair number of black and white images exist.
A P Tatt / Online Transport Archive

A Three Bridges to East Grinstead train, headed by M7 Class No.30055, runs into East Grinstead (High Level) station in February 1963. In the background an 'Oxted' diesel multiple unit can just be discerned; units of this type operated some services on this route almost from their introduction but steam was not entirely eclipsed on regular services until June 1965. The high level station at East Grinstead was completely erased from the landscape following the closure of the Three Bridges to Groombridge (Ashurst Junction) section of line and parts of the route in East Grinstead town centre were converted into a road. It should be noted that the service pattern on this line generally consisted of shuttle trains between Three Bridges and East Grinstead while the rest of the route was usually covered by through workings from London to Tunbridge Wells West. *Blake Paterson*

The last vestiges of the dreadful 1962/63 winter snows are still in evidence at Groombridge as H Class 0-4-4T No.31551 propels (what appears to be) an Oxted to Tunbridge Wells West train out of the station in February 1963. An unidentified bunker-first BR Standard Class 4MT 2-6-4T can just be discerned on the opposite track, possibly heading down the 'Cuckoo Line' to Eastbourne. The section of line through Groombridge was well documented by photographers due to it being one of the busiest stretches of largely steam-worked line on the SR. Trains radiated from nearby Tunbridge Wells West station to Oxted via Ashurst, London via Ashurst and East Grinstead, Brighton and Eastbourne and all used the section southwards as far as Groombridge Junction. Sadly, despite their location on the periphery of the capital, all of these services fell victim to the short-sighted transport policies of the 1960s and were closed as part of the supposed 'reshaping' of BR under the Beeching plan. Steam trains can still be observed at Groombridge, however, on the preserved Spa Valley line which operates from Tunbridge Wells to Eridge, where main line connections are available. *Roy Hobbs*

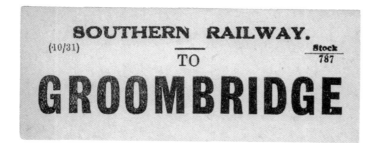

The chimney pots of Brighton. An unidentified BR Standard Class 4MT 2-6-4T, which appears to be in brand new ex-works condition, heads eastwards across London Road viaduct some time in 1955. Brighton works was still very much in business at this time and the 2-6-4T had presumably just been out-shopped – perhaps it was its very first outing! The photographer had luck on his side because the exhaust steam is being carried away from the engine and not obscuring it in any way. London Road viaduct, which dominates the area to the north-east of the station, was severely damaged by enemy action on 25th May 1943, and the line to the east cut, when two arches were totally destroyed. Regrettably, a railwayman was killed and a large amount of rolling stock damaged. A temporary steel bridge was installed, thus enabling trains to cross while new brick piers were being built. A branch was authorised from Brighton to Lewes as early as 1837 under the original London & Brighton Act, but the powers lapsed and it was left to the independent Brighton, Lewes & Hastings Railway (BLHR) to proceed with construction. This company had been incorporated under an Act of 1844 to construct a 32½ miles-long line linking Brighton with Bulverhythe (2¼ miles west of Hastings) via Lewes. The independent company was purchased by the LBSCR in 1845 and on 8th June 1846 the first section of line was opened as far as Friars Walk station in Lewes, the principal engineering work being the 330 yards-long London Road viaduct. Friars Walk was one of the original Lewes stations, used between 1846 and 1857, when new premises were built almost on the site of the present station. Remarkably, the rest of the line, as far as Bulverhythe, was opened on 27th June 1846, only a few weeks after the opening to Lewes, and this is probably explained by the fact that the heavy civil engineering works were concentrated between Brighton and Lewes. In 1845 the BLHR had obtained powers to extend its line along the coast from Bulverhythe to Ashford via Hastings while the hostile South Eastern Railway (SER) submitted a counter proposal for a line from Headcorn to Hastings via Tenterden. Parliament decided that the coastal route was preferable for strategic reasons but decreed that the SER was best placed to operate it, no doubt much to the annoyance of the LBSCR, the successor to the BLHR. The SER line from Ashford and LBSCR's short link from Bulverhythe were both scheduled to open on 13th February 1851 but the local SER staff refused to allow through running of 'Brighton' trains into Hastings station, claiming that they had no proof of the LBSCR's running powers. The SER even erected barriers across the tracks, and on one occasion apparently tore up the rails in order to deny the LBSCR access to Hastings. The 'Brighton' company speedily obtained an injunction against the SER but 'Brighton' trains were not permitted to stop at St Leonards until 1870.
J M Jarvis / Kidderminster Railway Museum

THE EAST COAST LINE

London Road viaduct is seen again on the extreme left of this shot as BR Standard 2-6-4T No.80037 accelerates up the rising 1 in 258 gradient towards Falmer with a Tonbridge train in the early 1960s. The building that can be seen immediately above the viaduct is Lovers Walk electric depot while in the background a further selection of Brighton's chimney pots can be discerned. This photograph was taken in the early 1960s. *Gerald Daniels*

THE EAST COAST LINE

A pair of former SECR C Class 0-6-0s, Nos.31686 and 31722, pass Kemp Town Junction heading eastwards on 28th April 1962. Both locomotives were withdrawn during that month and it is most likely that they were making their very last journey *en route* to Ashford works for breaking-up. It is recorded that both were cut-up within a few weeks, despite being in working order. The line on the left is the branch to Kemp Town which was still very much in use at the time of the photograph. *Gerald Daniels*

Brighton station, a focal point of routes in Sussex since the days of the LBSCR, is unquestionably the most impressive in Sussex but among the smaller stations Lewes stands out as an architectural masterpiece. The present station, part of which is seen here, dates from 1889 and was actually the third to be constructed in the town so it can be said that the railway history of Lewes would justify a book in its own right. The main entrance can be seen on the left of the picture and above it are octagonal ornaments, keyed arches and a splendid lantern sitting atop of the roof. The white-painted tower on the left houses the luggage lift. Note the track with platforms on both sides, an unusual feature found at only a few stations in the south of England; this was declared redundant when the line to Uckfield was closed in 1969 and has since been filled in. Sadly, the semaphore signals have also been made redundant since this photograph was taken. The train just creeping into the picture is a rail tour and this shot was taken in October 1962. *Charles Firminger*

Flooded out. The traditional bonfire night celebrations are a major event in Lewes, but 5th November 1960 will be remembered for altogether different reasons because parts of the town and much of its hinterland were under water after particularly heavy rainfall. This picture vividly illustrates the desperate situation at the south end of Lewes station where some trackwork had become completely submerged and as a result steam traction was pressed into use on local services, substituting for the more usual electric units that were unable to operate. The flood water at least provided some nice reflections that made this an attractive picture but the reflections were probably not appreciated by the general public whose travel plans were disrupted. Note the tracks of the erstwhile line to Uckfield curving away to the left. A train is signalled on the Eastbourne line and one wonders what type of engine was at the front end – a C Class engine worked at least one of the emergency passenger trains.
J J Smith / Bluebell Railway Museum

Who would have thought that a Stanier 'Jubilee' Class 4-6-0 from the London Midland Region (LMR) would ever be seen hauling an Eastbourne to Haywards Heath passenger train? But on 20th June 1964 that is exactly what happened when No.45672 *Anson* made history by working the 6.45pm Eastbourne to Romsey return special as far as Haywards Heath; it is seen here approaching Lewes. The train had been chartered by Messrs. Strong & Co of Romsey who were famous for their 'You are now entering the Strong country' pictorial signs along the Waterloo to Bournemouth line. The 'Jubilee' arrived at Newhaven on 19th June in charge of a car sleeper train from Glasgow, but failed and retired to Eastbourne shed which, by that date,

was the only shed in East Sussex available to steam traction, Brighton having closed a few days earlier. The following evening, amazingly, *Anson* was turned out to work the Haywards Heath leg of the special and one wonders how the crew reacted when told that a 'Jubilee' had been rostered for their train. The special reversed at Haywards Heath and was taken on by a Bulleid Pacific. It is thought that the operating authorities had, belatedly, become aware that 'Jubilees' were officially banned on the Central Division and No.45672 was reportedly dumped at the former Brighton shed while they deliberated on how it should be returned to the LMR. It eventually left for Willesden 'light engine' on 2nd July with a 20mph speed restriction but by that time had gained a place in Sussex railway folklore. The photographer was a railwayman and had presumably been given a 'tip off' about this unprecedented working. A sister locomotive, No.45617 *Mauritius* also worked into Sussex 'illegally' a few days later and this was also sent back 'light engine' at slow speed. *Charles Firminger*

Lewes has an intriguing and complicated railway history and many readers will probably be surprised to learn that this picture was actually taken in the town. The train is hidden away on the old goods lines near the site of one of the original stations: it appears to have reversed into the goods yard. The tracks on the right formed part of the original route through Lewes for passenger trains that was used between 1846, when the railway first arrived in the town, and the opening of the third station in 1889. The latter station remains in use today. The goods lines were retained and provided a valuable way of avoiding the new station, remaining in use until the late 1960s. The goods yard, and bridge carrying the Uckfield line across the goods lines, is obscured by the carriages. The locomotive is immaculate Maunsell N Class 'Mogul' No.31411 which was powering the 'Sussex Downsman' rail tour on 22nd March 1964. This engine was a favourite choice for rail tours at that time and maintained in impeccable condition by Redhill shed for such duties. *David Wigley*

The superb cloud formation, backdrop of downland, the meandering river Ouse with a sailing barge on the right and the striking contrast between the black locomotive and its train…this shot definitely has all the ingredients for a masterpiece and is one of the author's favourite Sussex photographs. The downland in the background is Cliffe Hill, which rises to 538ft above sea level, while the installation on the extreme right is the erstwhile Eastwoods cement works which closed in 1981. The location is between Lewes and Southerham Junction where the Seaford branch diverges from the main Eastbourne route and the train was apparently an empty stock working from Eardley carriage sidings, south London, to form a boat train from Newhaven Harbour to Victoria. The locomotive is Maunsell 'Schools' Class No.30915 *Brighton* and this photograph was taken on 26th September 1953. One wonders who sanctioned that ugly and intrusive pylon in such a sensitive location! *J J Smith / Bluebell Railway Museum*

A picture taken near Southerham Junction during the height of the floods on 5th November 1960. The photographer describes this working as a 'parcels train to Newhaven' and one is tempted to ask in the circumstances whether the town had been totally cut-off by the floods and the railway was the only means of conveying food parcels to the unfortunate inhabitants! The locomotive hauling the short train of

vans, which has just crossed over the river Ouse, is LBSCR E4 Class 0-6-2T No.32512. Note the lovely, puffy clouds – the weather conditions look so deceptive. The industrial branch to Eastwoods cement works is just out of view on the right. Originally the lime works of G. Newington & Co, it later became known as the Lewes Portland Cement Co until Eastwoods took over in 1929.
J J Smith / Bluebell Railway Museum

A rare photograph of a steam train substituting for an electric on the Brighton to Eastbourne line in 1955 during a national strike by enginemen. Not all the enginemen were involved, however, and the operating authorities clearly tried their best to run at least a token service using whatever resources were available. This train is the 3.30pm from Eastbourne to Lewes, powered by BR Standard Class 4MT 2-6-4T No.80015 pulling a three-coach 'Birdcage' set, and it is depicted leaving the quiet wayside station of Berwick. The crew were presumably trained only on steam traction and therefore unable to work an electric train. The siding on the left hand side served a local brickworks. The person visible by the lineside on the right is the late Sid Nash, a renowned railway photographer, who lived locally in Eastbourne. *J J Smith / Bluebell Railway Museum*

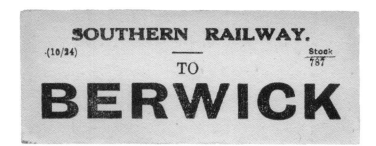

The WD Class 2-8-0s were the robust, unsung workhorses of heavy goods haulage and much more associated with long coal trains in the industrial north of England than leafy Sussex; however, 50 WD 2-8-0s were based on the SR in the very early post nationalisation days. Their bigger sisters, the WD Class 2-10-0s, also worked on the SR and there is photographic evidence of one working in Surrey, so it is likely they also visited Sussex. In this picture No.77256 wheels the 8.35am Three Bridges to Eastbourne goods along near Polegate on 29th March 1949. The locomotive, with air pumps prominent on the front and without a BR front number block on its smokebox door, makes a strange sight but nonetheless it is certainly earning its keep. No.77256 was built by the North British Locomotive Co of Glasgow in 1943 and loaned to the London & North Eastern Railway before being returned to the War Department in February 1945. In 1946 it was placed on loan to the Southern Railway, being based at Bricklayers Arms from 20th March of that year and was re-allocated to Hither Green from 13th December 1949; during its sojourn on the 'Southern' it received repairs at Brighton works. No.77256 was eventually taken into BR stock as No.90213, based at Goole shed, and lasted until 1966. *J J Smith / Bluebell Railway Museum*

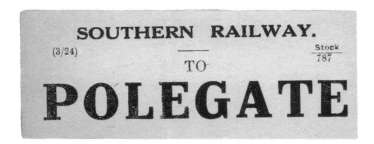

SOUTHERN RAILWAY.
(3/24)   Stock
                                                787
                          TO
POLEGATE

The Locomotive Club of Great Britain's 'Wealdsman' rail tour hauled by a brace of Maunsell 'Moguls', U Class No.31803 piloting N Class No.31411, takes the Stone Cross spur line at Polegate on 13th June 1965. This line gave a direct run from Polegate to Hastings, avoiding Eastbourne, and was originally the only route between the Eastbourne area and Hastings until the Stone Cross Junction to Willingdon Junction line was laid in 1871, thus enabling trains to run direct between Eastbourne and Hastings. The Stone Cross spur was officially closed from 6th January 1969 and the up track was lifted soon afterwards. The down line remained in place, however, and continued to be used sporadically for departmental trains. The junction at Polegate was removed in 1974, however, and the remaining single line served merely as an engineer's siding for some years thereafter with access from only the eastern end. The condemned coaches on the right had probably been dumped in a siding prior to breaking-up at Newhaven. Stone Cross Halt was located at the eastern end of the spur line beyond the main line junction but it was closed from 7th July 1935. *Roy Hobbs*

A view of the approach to Eastbourne station showing Maunsell N Class 2-6-0 No.31827 negotiating the layout with the 7.32am Wolverhampton (Low Level) to Hastings train on 27th July 1963. An unidentified locomotive is standing on the left apparently waiting to take the train on to Hastings. The signal box is partially visible on the right. *Graham Mallinson*

SOUTHERN RAILWAY.

(2/46) 48M

Stock
787

TO

EASTBOURNE

The International Union of Railways conference took place in Eastbourne in June 1951 and BR naturally put on a display of its latest equipment to impress the foreign dignitaries. The exhibits included BR Standard Class 5MT No.73001 and the Derby-built experimental BR/Fell 2-D-2 diesel mechanical locomotive No.10100. The latter was, perhaps, a rather strange choice and was far from a glittering success, being withdrawn after six years in service, though its failings were not known at the time. Pride of place at the display was, however, given to brand new 'Britannia' Class 7P/6F 'Pacific' No.70009 *Alfred the Great* which had just been released from Crewe works and was, therefore, in absolutely immaculate condition; it is seen here being shunted into position by an E4 Class tank locomotive that was still in 'Southern' livery. In addition to the modern items of rolling stock, signalling equipment and track components were also displayed and are depicted in this picture which was taken on 1st June 1951. One shudders to think how the representatives from continental railways reacted when the British officials informed them that BR was going to retain vacuum brakes as standard throughout the system. *J J Smith / Bluebell Railway Museum*

A BR Standard Class 4MT 2-6-4T locomotive, No.80152, stands at the buffer stops in Eastbourne station after arrival with the 12.32pm SO Hastings to Manchester Piccadilly train on 27th July 1963. Another locomotive would have been rostered for the next stage of the journey to Brighton where the train would have reversed once again. This part of Eastbourne station was sacrificed for a road improvement scheme in 1977 and a section of the station canopy removed; the number of operational platforms was reduced to three. On the left of the picture crowds of people can be seen alighting from a recent arrival, many of whom were no doubt holiday-makers looking forward to a fortnight by the sea. Note the former LMSR carriages which had probably been berthed at Hastings since the previous Saturday. *Graham Mallinson*

The location of this lovely little gem of a signal box is clear from the prominent nameboard on the front of the building; the box is thought to date from 1871 when the direct line from Eastbourne to Hastings was brought into use. This photograph was taken in early 1969 just before the Stone Cross spur line was taken out of regular use. *J J Smith / Bluebell Railway Museum*

The Gresley-designed coaches in this picture immediately suggest a train heading for the Eastern Region and, indeed, this is the 10.20am SO Hastings to Sheffield Victoria passing Pevensey & Westham station in the rain on 24th August 1963; motive power is provided by BR Standard Class 4MT 4-6-0 No.75068. This train, which ran for only five consecutive summer Saturdays, was routed along the old Great Central line via Woodford Halse, Rugby, Leicester and Nottingham and was booked to arrive in Sheffield at 5.44pm. This shot reveals the old up side station building and a gas light, on the right, that appears to have been left on. *Graham Mallinson*

2nd - SINGLE   SINGLE - 2nd
5345   5345
London Bridge or Victoria to
Lon. B'dge or Vic.   Lon. B'dge or Vic.
Bexhill Cen Cooden Beach   Bexhill Cen Cooden Beach
or Pevensey & Westham   or Pevensey & Westham
BEXHILL CENTRAL COODEN BEACH
or PEVENSEY & WESTHAM
Via Haywards Heath & Plumpton
(S)   110   FARE   17/0   (S)
For condit'ns see over   For condit'ns see over

The 12.30pm Hastings to Manchester (London Road) train passes St Leonards (West Marina) station on 16th September 1950. The engine shed is out of sight behind the train but part of a 'Schools' Class engine with its connecting rods removed can be seen on the left. The locomotive, No.32077, is of particular interest, being one of the I3 Class engines which were part of the Sussex railway scene for many years. A total of 27 was built between 1907 and 1913 for express passenger working and the engines weighed 76 tons and had 6ft 7½ in. driving wheels, but it should be noted that the prototype had some differences. The first example was withdrawn in 1944 while the rest of the class were wiped out by the introduction of Fairburn Class 4MT 2-6-4Ts in 1950/51, the only exception being No.32091 which lasted until June 1952. *J J Smith / Bluebell Railway Museum*

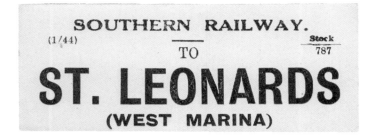

An unmistakable location. The distinctive backdrop of high ground, long bridge just visible through the mist, Victorian villas and trees immediately identify the location of this picture – is the station nameboard really essential? The train in the photograph is the 10.30am SO Birmingham (Snow Hill) to Hastings, hauled by BR Standard 2-6-4T No.80032, and this shot was taken on 24th August 1963. In the 1957 timetable this working left Birmingham ten minutes later and was booked to arrive in Hastings at 4.37pm, being routed via Reading, Guildford and Redhill. Needless to say, after leaving Guildford the train's progress was slow due to the need for time consuming reversals at Redhill, Brighton and Eastbourne. Passengers for Hastings must have wondered if they would ever arrive. The trackwork at this end of the station has been simplified following the removal of the up loop line which is now merely a bay accessible only from the eastern end of the station. *Graham Mallinson*

If there was ever a competition to find the most elaborate rail tour headboard ever used the Railway Correspondence & Travel Society (RCTS) would be a strong contender with this headboard and other decoration it produced for 'The Wealden Limited' which ran on 14th August 1955. This picture shows L Class 4-4-0 No.31764 simmering in Hastings station while some of the participants stand in admiration. The purpose of this tour was to mark the closure of the Lewes to East Grinstead 'Bluebell' line and it had originally been arranged to run on 12th June but had to be postponed due to a nationwide enginemen's strike. Surprisingly, when peace and normality returned to the railway system, BR agreed to run the tour on 14th August, after the 'Bluebell' line had been officially closed to all traffic, so one assumes that the RCTS had friends on BR in very high places. *J B C McCann / Online Transport Archive*

An interior view of Eastbourne shed taken on 25th March 1951 with nicely cleaned E4 Class No.2485 prominent. The shed at Eastbourne was built on land originally purchased by the LBSCR for a new carriage and wagon works and replaced a depot of the semi-roundhouse type sited near the station. The shed was opened in 1911 and had seven through roads that led to a 60ft diameter turntable. At one time it had as many as 40 engines on its books including some express passenger locomotives such as 'King Arthurs', 'Schools' and 'Brighton' Atlantics, but electrification of lines in the Eastbourne area in 1935 resulted in a huge decline in the shed's work. Even worse, during the Second World War several bombing raids left the depot virtually roofless and by the early 1950s it housed only a handful of locomotives for local goods duties plus passenger turns on the 'Cuckoo line' to Tunbridge Wells. The shed closed as an independent depot in 1952 but returned briefly to prominence after the closure of Brighton shed in June 1964. Ironically, this event coincided with an upsurge of inter-regional steam working, particularly on overnight car sleeper trains to Newhaven, and locomotives requiring servicing went to Eastbourne which had become the only point in east Sussex where this could be undertaken. On 26th June 1964 the shed boasted a quartet of 4-6-0s, Nos.44862, 45617, 61313 and 73159, the B1 Class engine having worked a train of pigeon vans to Lewes and then failed with a hot axle box. Within a year steam working in the area had been totally eliminated and the remains of Eastbourne shed were demolished in 1969.
J J Smith / Bluebell Railway Museum

EASTBOURNE MOTIVE POWER DEPOT

Eastbourne shed...going. BR Standard Class 4MT 2-6-4T No.80148, in quite clean condition, stands amid the ruins of the shed on 16th April 1961. The locomotive behind is C Class 0-6-0 No.31724 and other engines 'on shed' on that date included Q Class No.30534 and N Class 31829. *Charles Firminger*

Eastbourne shed gone...well, almost. This portrait of the shed was taken on 22nd June 1963 and one shudders to think what 'servicing' of locomotives or basic repair work would have been possible in such primitive conditions with no protection from the elements. BR Standard 2-6-4T No.80144, the engine nearest to the camera, remained at work in the Eastbourne area until the end of steam in June 1965 and hauled a BR-sponsored commemorative steam working over the 'Cuckoo' line on 12th June. Note that by the time of this photograph the shed's original seven roads had been reduced to just two. *David Wigley*

The vicissitudes of the Lewes to East Grinstead route (part of which is now known as the 'Bluebell Line') are well known and the fact that BR was forced to reinstate services after officially closing the line is quite remarkable. Colour pictures of the line in BR days are not plentiful because it was closed before colour photography became commonplace but, ironically, the preserved section has undoubtedly become one of the most photographed stretches of railway line in the world! Like all stations on the Lewes to East Grinstead route Newick & Chailey was a solidly built architectural gem with a striking porch at the front of the station, ornate chimneys and hanging tiles to keep out the worst of the weather. It was also unique because it was a three-storey building, this being dictated by the station's location in a cutting where space was at a premium. The living quarters were on the top floor, passenger facilities facing the forecourt on the middle floor while the basement was at platform level. The refreshment room was a popular facility with passengers and its closure in 1913 dealt a bitter blow to customers, particularly to local patrons and railway staff, who were henceforth forced to walk a mile to their nearest hostelry. The station ceased to be a crossing point in the 1930s and removal of the footbridge and up platform buildings did little to enhance its appearance. This picture was taken looking northwards on 16th March 1958, the day the line was finally closed, and everything of railway interest in this illustration has since been obliterated. *Charles Firminger*

The Bluebell Railway – making preservation history. BR steam traction throughout Sussex was very much in decline throughout the 1950s/60s but the establishment of the Bluebell Railway in 1960 ensured that at least a fragment of the county's steam heritage would survive. The line, the first preserved standard gauge passenger carrying railway in Great Britain, opened in August 1960 and soon won the affection of the general public, thus confounding the sceptics who opined that the whole idea of a line operated by volunteers was unrealistic and doomed to failure. Today, the railway has one of the most comprehensive collections of rolling stock outside the National Collection and is also among the most popular tourist attractions in Sussex. In March 2013 the railway achieved one of its major objectives when the extension to East Grinstead was completed. This shot was taken at Sheffield Park station on 7th August 1961, exactly a year after the line opened, and shows two former SECR P Class locomotives; No.323 is arriving with a train from Horsted Keynes (Bluebell Halt) while No.27 is waiting to leave with a northbound working. Note the marquee on the right, no doubt serving as a makeshift refreshment room. *The late Graham Hoare*

SOUTHERN RAILWAY.

(3/25)

Stock 787

TO

SHEFFIELD PARK

A portrait of beautifully turned out 'Brighton' Atlantic No.32426 *St. Alban's Head* awaiting departure from Horsted Keynes station with the Railway Correspondence & Travel Society's 'The Wealden Limited' rail tour on 14th August 1955. The train was run primarily to mark the closure of the Lewes to East Grinstead line and the date of the tour had been re-arranged due to an enginemen's strike but, actually, the journey over that line was only a small part of the itinerary. The train started from London Victoria and ran to Paddock Wood via Otford before running down to Hawkhurst and back. After returning to Paddock Wood it retraced its steps to Tonbridge before setting off to Hastings. The next stage of the tour took the train to Lewes, where it reversed, East Grinstead and eventually Victoria. Quite a day!
J B C McCann / Online Transport Archive

LEWES TO EAST GRINSTEAD

The LBSCR was always anxious to repel encroachment onto its territory by the SER and no doubt welcomed the opening of a branch from Three Bridges to East Grinstead in July 1855, and that from Lewes to Uckfield on 18th October 1858 which diverged from the main London line about 1½ miles north of Lewes. Both of these lines were promoted by independent companies which were soon taken over by the LBSCR. The LBSCR realised that East Grinstead and Uckfield were both within striking distance of Tunbridge Wells and was therefore keen to support the Brighton, Uckfield & Tunbridge Wells Railway, which had been incorporated in 1861, and another local concern that was intent on closing the gap between East Grinstead and Tunbridge Wells; the two routes converged at Groombridge with the line from there belonging to the Uckfield company. The route from East Grinstead opened in October 1866 while the extension from Uckfield was brought into use on 3rd August 1868. The latter involved long climbs up to a gable summit at which Crowborough, the principal intermediate station, is sited. Both of these lines were absorbed by the LBSCR before opening and the 'Brighton' company had thus achieved its aim of thwarting any incursions by the rival SER. It should be noted that on 1st October 1868 a new 3½ miles-long line was opened south of Barcombe Mills which provided independent access to Lewes, joining the 'East Coast' Brighton to Hastings line immediately east of Lewes station; the original route was abandoned. Here, the 9.38am Victoria to Brighton train is depicted leaving Barcombe Mills behind (what is thought to be) BR Standard 2-6-4T No.80059 on 17th February 1962. *Gerald Daniels*

SOUTHERN RAILWAY.
(11/32) TO Stock 787
BARCOMBE MILLS

Despite the generally cloudy conditions the photographer appears to have been lucky with the sun which popped out at just the right moment when Maunsell Q Class 0-6-0 No.30549 was shunting at Barcombe Mills station, also on 17th February 1962. No.30549 was very much the 'ugly duckling' of the Q class due to its somewhat unattractive stove-pipe chimney which was fitted in the mid-1950s following trials at Swindon works. Barcombe Mills station was situated in a rural location on the river Ouse and close to the village of Barcombe Cross; note the oil lamps and green painted station furniture so typical of 'Southern' practice. *Gerald Daniels*

Crowborough and Jarvis Brook station is seen in this picture which was taken on 24th November 1968, a considerable time after BR steam traction in Sussex had been eclipsed, but it had not been substantially changed during the intervening period. The station presents an attractive, balanced appearance with buildings and canopies intact on both platforms and is, of course, provided with a set of BR 'sausage' signs and gas lamps; this view is looking towards Eridge. The usual regional green and cream colours are to the fore; painting that long fence on the left must have been a tedious job for the painters. Crowborough station is remote from many districts of the town and commuters probably find it more convenient (and cheaper!) to drive to Eridge. *Gerald Daniels*

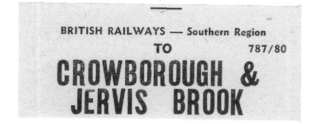

Railway photographers are always full of complaints about the fickle British climate and the weather's tendency to ruin a 'master shot' when the sun is obscured just at the wrong moment. But here is a photograph of BR Standard Class 4MT 4-6-0 No.75074 leaving Eridge in full sun as a huge area of dark cloud hovers menacingly overhead – could the photographer have wished for more dramatic conditions? What is more, there is a fine display of autumn tints in this picture that was taken on 29th October 1961. The train is the 12.55pm Suo Brighton to Victoria. *John Langford*

Silver birch trees enhance this photograph of a D1 Class 4-4-0 (which is thought to be No.31489) pictured near the former High Rocks Halt, between Tunbridge Wells West and Groombridge stations, on 5th March 1960. The halt served a picturesque outcrop of sandstone rock and was opened in 1907 principally for leisure traffic; it was closed for a period during the Second World War and then completely from 5th May 1952. *John Langford*

Burnished and polished to perfection, yet a few weeks after this portrait was taken on 13th April 1958 *Beachy Head* was broken-up; what an unforgivable tragedy! No.32424, which was built at Brighton in 1911, outlasted its sister engines by eighteen months and had become very much a celebrity machine, being the last surviving 'Atlantic' in BR service. Unfortunately, Brighton shed had little regular work for the engine and it spent a lot of time in store in between sorties on the lightweight Brighton to Bournemouth train and other duties that were not too strenuous. Prior to withdrawal it made a commemorative last run between Victoria and Newhaven, a route with which this legendary class had been associated for many years, and reportedly touched 70mph crossing the Ouse viaduct – not bad for an old timer. *Beachy Head* is seen here at Newhaven Town station after completing its run from Victoria. Later in the day the tour was hauled from Newhaven to Brighton by BR Standard 2-6-4T No.80154, the last locomotive built at Brighton works, and returned to London behind a 'King Arthur' Class locomotive. On 24th April *Beachy Head* hauled an empty stock train from Lancing works to Micheldever and then made its last journey to Eastleigh works for cutting-up, a sad loss to the railway preservation movement which was just starting to gather strength. The Lewes to Newhaven section of the Seaford branch was opened to passenger traffic from 8th December 1847 while the extension onwards to Seaford opened on 1st June 1864. *Derek Penney*

Back in the days before the nation was gripped by Health & Safety mania railway enthusiasts were often able to wander around railway installations at will as exemplified here by this picture taken at Newhaven shed on 13th April 1958. Everybody knew the dangers and most folk acted accordingly. Here dozens of soberly dressed rail aficionados can be seen standing around the unguarded, white-painted turntable pit and walking on the turntable which presumably provided a better spot for photographers. The locomotives on view (from left to right) are BR Standard 2-6-4T No.80154 (partially visible), 'Terrier' No.32636 in the middle of the picture and *Beachy Head*, approaching the shed which is behind the photographer. Part of Newhaven Town station, the signal box and adjacent crossing gates, and the glorious South Downs on the horizon complete the scene. *J B C McCann / Online Transport Archive*

SOUTHERN RAILWAY.
Issued subject to the Bye-laws, Regulations &
Conditions in the Company's Bills and Notices.

6768   **Newhaven Town to**   6768
Newhaven Town   Newhaven Town
Newhaven Hr.   Newhaven Hr.
NEWHAVEN HARBOUR
THIRD CLASS   THIRD CLASS
Fare 2d.   Fare 2d.
NOT TRANSFERABLE.

THE SEAFORD BRANCH

There were many aspects to Newhaven's railway heritage which encompassed three separate stations, a locomotive shed, rolling stock scrap yard and civil engineer's tip, but the most fascinating installation of all was undoubtedly the West Quay tramway. It ran from just north of Newhaven Town station and crossed the river Ouse on a swing bridge before running along the west bank of the river and on to a long breakwater. It was laid in about 1879 when much needed improvements to the harbour were being undertaken, and its original purpose was to carry materials for the construction of the breakwater and lighthouse which were being built as part of the Newhaven Harbour Company's plan to create a non-tidal port. Later, the tramway was used to convey materials for breakwater maintenance and in addition it served a tarpaulin and rope works, but in its closing years the tramway's principal function was to serve a BR engineers' yard. The operation of the West Quay line was monopolised by diminutive A1X Class 'Terrier' locomotives, the only class permitted on the lightly laid track, and these engines were an almost daily sight for decades as they scuttled across the bridge, delaying waiting motorists. In this picture No.32670 is seen at the entrance to the engineers' yard in August 1962 while a couple of local lads with time to spare stare at the photographer and wonder what all the fuss is about. *Roy Hobbs*

A wooden drawbridge crossed the river Ouse until it was replaced by a swing bridge in 1866. The span took about three minutes to open, then there would be another frustrating ten minute delay while a vessel passed and a further three minutes to close the bridge, so it would be an understatement to say that it was not popular with motorists. The only alternative main road river crossing was some miles upstream at Lewes, so most drivers opted to endure the long wait while a ship passed. The queue of traffic often brought the town centre to a complete standstill so it probably came as a huge relief when the old bridge was replaced by a new high level structure in 1976. In this picture 'Terrier' No.32678 is depicted crossing the swing bridge on 30th July 1963. *R C Riley*

You have been warned. In Victorian times every item of railway equipment was built to last and this delightful trespass notice had certainly stood the all important test of time. This picture was taken on the West Quay line during the summer of 1963. One wonders if this marvellous collector's item survived and where it might be today. *J J Smith / Bluebell Railway Museum*

Dwarfed by the cliffs towering above it, A1X Class 0-6-0T No.32678 reverses a short train around the chalk headland near the entrance to the breakwater which extended a quarter of a mile out to sea. There was a store for building materials here, and a short siding, but there was no run round loop and wagons had to be fly shunted. On a bad winter's day conditions at this exposed spot could be really nasty. This picture was taken on 30th July 1963 shortly before closure and it is possible this train was worked as far as the headland for unofficial photographic purposes – BR motive power inspectors are unlikely to have been thick on the ground at this remote spot! The line was closed completely on 10th August 1963 when the last wagons were cleared away by No.32678 and a fascinating part of Newhaven's considerable transport history was no more. *Trevor Owen / R C Riley collection*

Ferocious gradients, tortuous curvature, delightful Wealden scenery and some of the finest station buildings to be found anywhere are attributes for which the Eastbourne to Tunbridge Wells line will probably be best remembered. This lovely route was universally known as the 'Cuckoo Line' and derived its name from the Cuckoo Fair which takes place every April in Heathfield. The route was opened in three distinct stages, the first section from Polegate, on the LBSCR's Brighton to Hastings line, to the market town of Hailsham opening on 14th May 1849. This first stretch of the line was only three miles long and Hailsham was destined to remain a terminus for some time. In 1864 the South Eastern Railway (SER), anxious to obtain a share of the lucrative Eastbourne traffic, proposed a line from the London area to Eastbourne that would have sliced through what the LBSCR regarded as its territory and in retaliation the latter proposed the Ouse Valley Railway from south of Balcombe to Hailsham via Uckfield. Two years later a series of bank failures caused many schemes for new railways throughout Great Britain to be abandoned. Nothing further happened until 1873 when a local company was formed to construct a three-foot gauge line between Hailsham and Tunbridge Wells which developed into a scheme for a standard gauge line under the auspices of the 'South Eastern'. Perhaps it should be noted that the original proposed gauge of this line is disputed by some historians. The promoters struggled to raise the necessary capital, however, and the LBSCR was able to obtain an Act to take over the powers on payment of £8,534. After years of delay work began, the contractor being Joseph Firbank & Sons, and by February 1880 was sufficiently advanced for an inspection to be carried out by the Officers of the LBSCR. The section north of Hailsham, as far as Heathfield, was brought into use on 3rd April 1880 while the final stretch to Redgate Mill Junction, on the Uckfield to Tunbridge Wells line, opened on 1st September of the same year. The 'Cuckoo Line' diverged from the Eastbourne to Brighton route at Polegate and in this photograph the 5.56pm Eastbourne to Tunbridge Wells West train is seen departing behind J1 Class 4-6-2T No.32325 on 27th July 1950. This locomotive, built at Brighton in 1910, was the first express passenger tank engine of that wheel arrangement to be built in Great Britain and it worked, together with J2 Class sister engine No.32326, on the Brighton line until electrification in 1933. Thereafter they had a much more sedate life based at Tunbridge Wells West shed and both of these non-standard machines finished their working lives in mid-1951. Apart from the two running lines and station building on the extreme left, none of the railway infrastructure seen in this picture survives today because Polegate station now occupies a new site to the west. Note that trains on the 'Cuckoo Line' used only the outer faces of the two island platforms. This picture was taken from the steps of Polegate West signal box which most local enthusiasts of the day would have claimed to be among the best, if not *the* best, viewpoints in the town! *J J Smith / Bluebell Railway Museum*

A LMSR-designed Fairburn Class 4MT 2-6-4T, No.42100, drifts downhill into Polegate with the 11.08am Victoria to Eastbourne train on a snowy 16th December 1950. The train is formed of a 'Birdcage' 3-set of coaches which would not have taxed this powerful locomotive even on the heavy grades of the 'Cuckoo Line'. No.42100 was a product of Brighton works from where it emerged in August 1950 so it was almost brand new at the time of this photograph. *J J Smith / Bluebell Railway Museum*

The market town of Hailsham was one of the few medium sized population centres on the Eastbourne to Tunbridge Wells line but it was quite close to Eastbourne and buses probably creamed off most of the local passenger traffic. Here, on 11th June 1965, just three days before the final curtain came down on this lovely line as a through route, an unidentified bunker-first BR Standard 2-6-4T awaits departure with an Eastbourne train. Note there is also a train in the up platform. A shuttle service to and from Eastbourne served Hailsham for a further three years after closure of the rest of the line to passengers. *The late Graham Hoare*

Hellingly – an unmistakable location. Latterly there was no passing loop at Hellingly, the only station on the 'Cuckoo Line' without this facility, so it is immediately recognisable even by those without a detailed knowledge of the route. In some respects it was the most interesting station on the line because the short electrified line to Hellingly Hospital started from here, the interchange sidings once occupied the waste ground on the right of the picture. Further information about the hospital railway can be found on p.112. This photograph depicts Maunsell 'Mogul' No.31400, powering the 8.08am Tonbridge to Eastbourne train, pulling away from Hellingly on 8th April 1964. *David Clark*

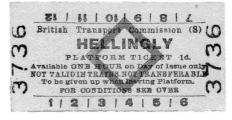

The Locomotive Club of Great Britain's 'Wealdsman' rail tour ran on 13th June 1965 to commemorate the closure of the 'Cuckoo Line' and also the Horsham to Guildford branch. The train's route was quite ingenious and also included the Three Bridges to Groombridge (Ashurst Junction) and Steyning lines both of which were under threat of closure at that time and, indeed, were subsequently abandoned. In this picture the rail tour is seen passing Horam station behind a brace of Maunsell 'Moguls', U Class No.31803 (leading) and N Class No.31411. Note the diesel unit in the adjacent platform. *The late Graham Hoare*

An everyday scene at Heathfield with a BR Standard Class 4MT 2-6-4T carrying out a little shunting; a May 1965 photograph. The locomotive was apparently working a pick-up goods down the line from Tunbridge Wells. *Blake Paterson*

A feature of the last few days of operations on the 'Cuckoo Line' was drivers' names chalked on the front of various locomotives. No.80089, depicted here entering Heathfield on 11th June 1965 with a northbound train, had been unofficially christened 'Earl Sellewood' while sister engine No.80144 bore the name 'Lord William Bryant'. It must have been quite a surprise, and certainly a great honour, for a local driver to find himself elevated to the House of Lords! *David Wigley*

Two members of BR staff chat on the down platform at Heathfield on 3rd June 1962 as former SECR H Class 0-4-4T No.31518 simmers gently before departing with a southbound working to Eastbourne. Like all stations on the line, Heathfield was sturdily built but differed from other stations on the route because the main building was on a higher level than the platforms adjacent to a road bridge; both are visible in the background. During the station's early years the borehole from where water was pumped often ran dry during a long spell of weather without rain, this being largely due to Heathfield's elevated position. An unusual incident occurred in 1896 when natural gas was discovered during work to deepen the borehole and the station lighting was converted to burn natural gas. *David Clark*

SOUTHERN RAILWAY.

(6/30)   Stock
                    TO   787

HEATHFIELD

7 | 8 | 9 | 10 | 11 | 12

BRITISH RAILWAYS (S)
HEATHFIELD
PLATFORM TICKET 1d.
Available ONE HOUR on DAY of ISSUE ONLY
NOT VALID IN TRAINS NOT TRANSFERABLE
To be given up when leaving Platform
FOR CONDITIONS SEE BACK.

1 | 2 | 3 | 4 | 5 | 6

3006   3006

2nd - SINGLE   SINGLE - 2nd

Horam to

Horam   Horam
Heathfield   Heathfield

HEATHFIELD

(S)   9d. Fare 9d.   (S)

For conditions see over   For conditions see over

6347   6347

The 4.39pm Eastbourne to Tunbridge Wells West train, powered by former LBSCR D3 Class 0-4-4T No.32385, is depicted near Mayfield in the early 1950s. These locomotives were constructed between 1892 and 1896 for outer suburban duties and a total of 36 was built; this particular example was out-shopped in December 1893 and formerly named *Portsmouth*. The engines were equipped with pull-push apparatus from 1933 onwards. When BR came into being in 1948 it inherited a total of 28 locomotives of this class but this number was quickly reduced as the modern LMSR-designed Fairburn 2-6-4Ts became available and by the end of 1953 only one representative, No.32390, survived and outlasted its sister engines by almost two years. *J J Smith / Bluebell Railway Museum*

On the ticket:

British Transport Commission (S)

ROTHERFIELD & MARK CROSS
PLATFORM TICKET 2d.
Available one hour on day of issue only.
Not valid in trains. Not transferable.
To be given up when leaving platform
For conditions see over

2340

Perhaps the most remarkable thing about Rotherfield and Mark Cross station is the fact that at some stage it was equipped with electric lighting, as the lamp standards seen in this June 1965 picture bear testament. Incredibly, it also had a refreshment room at one time. Like all 'Cuckoo Line' stations Rotherfield was simply magnificent – a true architectural masterpiece – and the station's tranquil setting undoubtedly added to its appeal. Regrettably, like so many country stations it was sited a fair distance from the villages it purported to serve, both being well over a mile away and, in the case of Rotherfield, also 160ft higher than the village so prospective passengers without their own transport were faced with a considerable uphill walk. The South signal box can just be seen in the distance at the end of the down platform but, amazingly, at one stage Rotherfield enjoyed the luxury of two boxes, the North box having closed in 1935. The summit of the 'Cuckoo Line' was between Mayfield and Rotherfield near Argos Hill which is on the 605ft contour so this gives some idea of the height gained since leaving the coast. There was a tortuous descent from Argos Hill to Rotherfield on a 1 in 50 gradient so drivers had to keep their hand firmly on the brake handle. *The late Graham Hoare*

EASTBOURNE TO TUNBRIDGE WELLS

An example of the almost indestructible cast iron SR notices which were a very common sight throughout the system; this specimen was photographed near Rotherfield on 11th June 1965. *J J Smith / Bluebell Railway Museum*

The signalman at Redgate Mill Junction, where the 'Cuckoo Line' diverged from the Tunbridge Wells to Crowborough route just south of Eridge, holds up the staff, presumably for the photographer's benefit. Working in this relatively isolated signal box must have been a lonely job at times but for those who enjoyed peace and quiet it was probably ideal, surrounded by delightful Wealden scenery. The gentle sounds of the countryside were another bonus, only occasionally interrupted by passing trains and then only for a brief period! In addition, provided one pulled the right lever at the right time(!) it was a posting that meant you were largely your own boss away from interfering members of BR management. The box here dated from 1894 when the 'main' Crowborough line was doubled. Hitherto there had been two parallel single lines south of Eridge since 1880 when the 'Cuckoo Line' was opened to Heathfield, but no physical connection at Redgate Mill. This picture was taken on 8th August 1962. *J J Smith / Bluebell Railway Museum*

Most principal railway routes in the south of England had their distinguishing characteristics, the Waterloo to Exeter line was known for its relatively high speeds, the Brighton line for heavy commuter traffic while the Victoria to Dover Marine route was identified with the famous 'Golden Arrow' boat train. The Hastings line, however, was notorious because of the restricted width of its tunnels which gave the civil engineer's dept. a headache and have plagued operations since the day the route opened. The South Eastern Railway (SER) reached Tonbridge via Redhill in May 1842 and work commenced on the 4¾ miles-long branch to Tunbridge Wells in 1844, this eventually opening throughout on 25th November 1846. The rest of the Hastings line followed in stages a few years later, the 15¼ miles to Robertsbridge opening on 1st September 1851, the next six miles as far as Battle on New Year's Day 1852 while the final stretch down to Bopeep Junction, just outside Hastings, was brought into use on 1st February 1852. This delightfully named junction apparently took its name from a nearby, ancient tavern where shepherds used to gather. Problems with the tunnels on

the line became apparent in March 1855 when a section of brickwork in Mountfield tunnel collapsed and additional layers of bricks had to be inserted by the SER to strengthen its lining. Examination of Grove and Strawberry Hill tunnels, just south of Tunbridge Wells, revealed very poor workmanship and in the case of Grove tunnel it was found that only one layer of bricks had been used instead of the four specified. The SER took out an action against the contractors only to discover that one of the main culprits had fled the country! Remedial work was carried out but this had the effect of reducing the width of the tunnels and clearance problems became acute in later years as rolling stock increased in length. This was not the end of the saga because, in September 1949, cracks started to appear in Bopeep tunnel which necessitated its closure for six months with trains from Charing Cross to Hastings being diverted to Bexhill West. The problems with tunnels have tended to overshadow other aspects of the line which is blessed with some particularly attractive Wealden scenery and, in steam days, the route's tortuous nature and heavy gradients always provided a challenge for enginemen. The introduction of the 'Schools' class 4-4-0s on the route in the early 1930s revolutionised services along the route and these engines held sway on the heavier trains until dieselisation. Unfortunately, the early dieselisation of the line's passenger trains in 1957/58 meant that relatively few pictures were submitted for publication in this album – railway photographers were not inclined to wait around for hours in the hope that a goods train might appear. This picture was taken at Battle Road Crossing which adjoined the former Mountfield Halt, south of Robertsbridge. The gates were manually operated by the crossing keeper who lived in the adjacent property and was also expected to issue tickets to passengers – note the ticket window to the right of the 'departures' notice. Mountfield Halt was built in 1923 but was relatively short-lived, closing from 6th October 1969.
J J Smith / Bluebell Railway Museum

Robertsbridge station is, of course, best known as the southern terminus of the Kent & East Sussex Railway (KESR), but the station itself has some interesting history. Amazingly, the establishment once had no fewer than four wagon turntables while at one time there was an elevated water tank on the up platform that had a small glasshouse as an extension to its base! In the early 1960s a preservation scheme for the KESR was getting underway and various items of rolling stock were berthed in the goods yard which took on the air of a museum and became a place of pilgrimage for enthusiasts. This picture of Robertsbridge station was taken on 12th April 1958; two months later the full Hastings line diesel service was introduced and steam on regular passenger duties was consigned to the history books. *Charles Firminger*

The connection to the KESR was at the north end of Robertsbridge station and can be seen in this illustration of Maunsell U1 Class 'Mogul' No.31902 arriving with a Hastings-bound train on 12th June 1957. Many trains on the Hastings Line conveyed a Pullman car which, in this case, is the fourth vehicle in the formation. The date of this picture is particularly significant because the first stage of the Hastings line dieselisation was due to come into operation from 17th June and the photographer presumably wanted to witness operations on the line while it was still monopolised by steam traction. In fact, resulting from a catastrophic signal box fire at Cannon Street station, three diesel units had entered service earlier than planned so not all trains may have been steam worked on the day of his visit. The vehicle in the yard on the right appears to be a ferry van and one wonders what on earth a vehicle of that type was doing in Robertsbridge goods yard!
Mike Esau

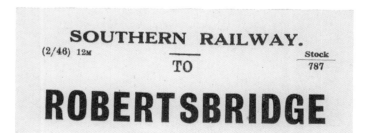

An unidentified 'Schools' Class locomotive in black livery heads southwards from Wadhurst some time in the late 1950s. Note the train's formation which includes passenger vehicles in carmine and cream, a Pullman car and, right on the end, a coach in green livery – quite an assortment. *Ken Wightman*

Another Hastings-bound train is seen at Wadhurst, this time with a green-liveried 'Schools' Class engine in charge, No.30908 *Westminster*, an Eastleigh product dating from July 1930. Once again, the train is formed of a motley collection of carriages, the one immediately behind the locomotive in red livery being a former SECR ten compartment non-corridor third, a type of coach noted for their uncomfortable, hard seats. Behind that is (what appears to be) one of the 'continental' coaches ordered by the SECR but delivered mainly in 'Southern' days, while the rest of the train comprises two Maunsell 3-sets, the first in carmine and cream while the set in the rear is in traditional SR green. This picture was taken on an unknown date in the late 1950s. *Ken Wightman*

Three young train spotters admire Maunsell 'Schools' Class 4-4-0 No.30924 *Haileybury* as it approaches Wadhurst with a Hastings train on 12th June 1957. The station is located about a mile from the village but is adjacent to the Tunbridge Wells road along which a local bus is proceeding northwards. The photographer pressed the shutter at just the right moment to capture the bus in his picture or, perhaps, it was just very good luck! Wadhurst station is the summit of the line and crews of northbound trains must have breathed a deep sigh of relief because it marked the end of the almost ten miles-long climb from Robertsbridge. *Mike Esau*

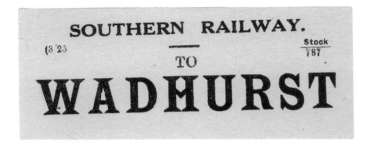

SOUTHERN RAILWAY.

(3 '25   Stock 787

TO

WADHURST

The 4½ miles-long Bexhill West branch was built to link the town with the main line at Crowhurst and reduced the distance from London to Bexhill by rail from 72 miles, on the LBSCR's route, to 62 miles. The SECR was anxious to obtain a share of the Bexhill traffic and the bill for construction of the line was sanctioned by Parliament in 1897, construction commencing in January of the following year. In the event the branch took four years to complete due to the exceptionally heavy earthworks involved as well as a substantial 17 arch viaduct which took the line across the Combe Haven valley. The SECR had high expectations for the line when it opened on 1st June 1902 and through expresses to both Charing Cross and Cannon Street were provided. Rather strangely, the branch opened on a Sunday without the fanfare that usually accompanies such events and it is thought that the low key launch was deliberate in order to avoid further upsetting the rival LBSCR which previously had had the monopoly of the Bexhill traffic, though there had been considerable celebration at a private ceremony the previous day. The 'Brighton' company's dominant position was never really challenged, however, this being due in large part to the ideal location of (what later became) Bexhill Central station. Electrification in 1935 reinforced the status of the former 'Brighton' route and passenger traffic on the Bexhill West branch suffered, latterly consisting principally of city gentlemen commuters while local passengers during the day were sparse, apart from schoolchildren. The line was closed from 14th June 1964 and it is reported that some of the travellers on the last train had also been passengers on the first, 62 years previously. The line's promoters were clearly eternal optimists and two island platforms were built at Bexhill West but latterly one had become very overgrown. In this shot the sunshine creates an attractive pattern of shadows on the platform surface as H Class 0-4-4T No.31520 waits to leave with a shuttle train to Crowhurst on 30th March 1957. *John Langford*

THE BEXHILL WEST BRANCH

The 1.30pm Charing Cross to Bexhill West train, with Maunsell 'Schools' 4-4-0 No.30928 *Stowe* in charge, is seen just south of Crowhurst Junction on 3rd June 1950. This train was one of a number run between 27th November 1949 and 4th June 1950 to compensate for the withdrawal of services to Hastings due to the prolonged closure of Bopeep tunnel while it was being relined. The introduction of this emergency service doubtless reminded older, regular travellers of the halcyon days when a through Charing Cross service was provided on a regular basis, but that ceased running in 1940. Note the very deep cutting at this point which illustrates the heavy earthworks required during the line's construction. *J J Smith / Bluebell Railway Museum*

There had been a scheme in 1864 to connect Cranbrook with the historic town of Tenterden but this foundered and nothing further was pursued until 1896. That year saw the formation of the Rother Valley (Light) Railway Co. (RVR) which gained authorisation under the 1896 Light Railway Act to construct a branch from the SER's main line Robertsbridge station to Rolvenden (then called Tenterden). This lightly laid, independent 12 miles-long route, run by Colonel H F Stephens, opened on 2nd April 1900 and its initial rolling stock consisted of just two locomotives and six coaches. The RVR had plans to extend and these came to fruition on 15th April 1903 when it opened an extension to the main SECR line at Headcorn. In 1904 the company announced further plans for another extension, this time to Maidstone, and changed its name to the more grandiose title of Kent & East Sussex Railway (KESR). The Maidstone idea did not materialise, however, and the KESR gained a reputation as a rather eccentric, ramshackle concern, this being underlined by its remarkable collection of secondhand steam locomotives and rolling stock, obtained from various sources, that littered Rolvenden yard. Early in the 1930s the Tenterden to Headcorn section started to lose money and the line went into receivership in 1932 and, to make matters even worse, Colonel Stephens died in 1933. Despite these reverses the independent KESR managed to hang on throughout the Second World War and became part of the BR network in 1948. The writing was clearly on the wall, however, and in January 1954 BR withdrew the passenger service and closed completely the northern section of line beyond Tenterden. Goods traffic was withdrawn in June 1961. But that event, of course, merely marked the end of one chapter in the line's chequered history! A train for Tenterden headed by former LBSCR 'Terrier' 0-6-0T No.32670, poses in the bay platform at Robertsbridge on 29th July 1953; note that this is a mixed train conveying both passenger accommodation and goods traffic. No.32670, originally built at Brighton in 1872, had a very long association with this line going back to 1901 when it was bought by the RVR, becoming No.3 *Bodiam. G W Powell / R C Riley collection*

A conveniently sited footbridge on Robertsbridge station provided the perfect grandstand for photographers and in this view 'Terrier' No.32678 simmers in the bay platform with a hop pickers' train to Bodiam on 14th September 1957. This is an instance where passenger trains continued to operate on a seasonal basis long after the government had officially sanctioned their withdrawal! Note the accommodation provided for the unfortunate guard, a four wheeled brake van sandwiched between two ten-compartment third coaches – presumably nothing more luxurious was available. The goods yard seems to have been really busy at this time judging by the number of wagons in the picture. On the right one of the (then) brand new six-car diesel units enters the station with a train for Charing Cross. *Edwin Wilmshurst*

Another shot of a mixed train on the KESR, this time with 'Terrier' 0-6-0T No.32655 in charge. This scene was recorded on 28th July 1953 and shows the train heading away from Robertsbridge near Northbridge Street level crossing. No.32655 can be seen at the time of writing at the Bluebell Railway but it is not currently operational. After being derelict for many years this section has since been rebuilt by a preservation group and it is possible that one day regular services will be restored, providing a link with the existing Bodiam to Tenterden line. Here's hoping! *G W Powell / R C Riley collection*

Preservation history. In early 1965 the scheme to preserve the KESR was still in its infancy and, like most fledgling preservation enterprises, suffered from a shortage of funds, manpower and covered accommodation for rolling stock. Occasionally, provided a serviceable locomotive was available, a train would gingerly venture down from Rolvenden along the moribund section of line and here 0-6-0ST No.14 *Charwelton*, in somewhat dilapidated condition, is depicted at Northiam on 17th January 1965 in charge of a single four wheel coach and wagon – just the kind of scene that would have delighted Colonel Stephens. *Charwelton* was a Manning Wardle product dating from 1917. The appearance of No.14 probably raised a few eyebrows among the 'locals' and really must have startled motorists as it crossed the nearby main road.
The late Graham Hoare

SOUTHERN RAILWAY.
Issued subject to the Bye-laws, Regulations &
Conditions in the Company's Bills and Notices.

Tenterden Town to

Tenterden Town   Tenterden Town
Northiam   Northiam

NORTHIAM

THIRD CLASS   THIRD CLASS
Fare 1/8   Fare 1/8
NOT TRANSFERABLE.

0003

Table 24   Week Days

Table 24   ROBERTSBRIDGE, TENTERDEN TOWN, and HEADCORN
Third class only

[Timetable table — Down and Up services, Week Days only]

A Saturdays only. Runs until 30th May, 1953.
B Via Redhill (Tables 29 and 40). Arr. Cannon St., 6 55 p.m. on Sats.
H Arr. 11 25 a.m until 1st November, 1952, and again commencing 30th March, 1953.
M Stops by signal to set down or pick up passengers
N Saturdays only. Commences 6th June, 1953.
SX Saturdays excepted
U Station for Beckley and Sandhurst
Z Arrives 6 38 p.m. until 1st November, 1952, and again commencing 4th April, 1953.

Counties such as Yorkshire and Co Durham were always a happy hunting ground for devotees of industrial steam locomotives but Sussex, where one of the main industries is tourism, had very little to offer. Most industrial activity, such as it was, was concentrated in the eastern half of the county at locations such as Eastbourne gas works and Eastwoods cement works near Lewes. It is debatable whether former SECR P Class 0-6-0T No.31556, originally built at Ashford works in February 1909, qualifies as an industrial locomotive and it was certainly a late arrival on the scene. When the KESR line was closed in June 1961 the owner of Messrs. Hodson, flour millers, of Northbridge Street, between Robertsbridge and Salehurst, decided that he wished to maintain rail traffic and purchased No.31556, the last survivor on BR which had just been withdrawn, for shunting duties between the mill and Robertsbridge station.

The P class engine was noted at Brighton shed, crudely repainted without visible signs of ownership, on 12th June 1961 and ran 'light engine' to Robertsbridge two days later. No.31556 is depicted at the mill in October 1964 looking very much the worse for wear after prolonged exposure to the elements. When it was delivered the mill owner apparently stated his intention to name the engine *Pride of Sussex* and newly applied paint on the bunker probably represented the first stage of No.31556's repainting and subsequent naming which had been completed by May 1965. The mill owner's decision to purchase the locomotive ensured its long term survival – it is now preserved on the Kent & East Sussex Railway. *R C Riley*

The gypsum mine at Mountfield began life in 1876 when the Sub-Wealden Gypsum Company started mining and laid a one mile-long branch from the Hastings to Tunbridge Wells main line. It is one of the largest rail-served industrial installations in Sussex and for some years steam traction was employed to move wagons between the exchange sidings with BR and the works. This picture shows 0-6-0ST *Kemp* undertaking some shunting on 13th August 1965; this engine was built by Andrew Barclay (works no. 2241) in 1948 so it was quite a modern machine. *David Wigley*

The Hastings to Ashford line was originally proposed by the Brighton, Lewes & Hastings Railway (BLHR) and this company obtained the necessary powers in 1845 during the years of 'railway mania' which saw hundreds of parliamentary bills deposited for proposed new lines. Parliament later changed its mind (as previously mentioned) and decided that the SER was better placed to operate the route, and this created an unpleasant situation on the opening day, 13th February 1851, when the LBSCR (which had absorbed the BLHR) and rival SER tried to delay each other's trains. Their actions reportedly included holding up trains at Bopeep Junction for long periods, tearing up track and placing barriers across station approach roads in what was later dubbed the 'second battle of Hastings'. The LBSCR agent was even marooned in his office for a period, so things must have got really nasty. The Hastings to Ashford line crosses the completely level Romney marsh but there are gradients at each end; one of the most notable civil engineering features is the 1,402 yards-long Ore tunnel. Remarkably, this shot is the only 'publishable' colour picture of an ordinary timetabled steam train at Hastings station ever seen by the author, so it seems to be quite a rarity! Clearly, Hastings station was not favoured by colour photographers in the days of steam. The train illustrated is the 6.52pm to Ashford, hauled by L1 Class 4-4-0 No.31754, and this picture was taken on 4th June 1958. *Charles Firminger*

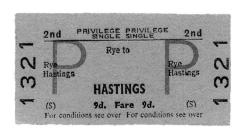

The 5.45am London Bridge to Hastings train was one of those peculiar workings that fascinated railway aficionados because, upon arrival at Hastings, part of the train changed its identity and worked forward at 8.32am to Ashford so, in effect, it was a through London Bridge to Ashford train via Hastings! Here Maunsell 'Schools' Class 4-4-0 No.30923 *Bradfield* waits at Rye before setting off on the final stage of its journey to Appledore and Ashford on 14th April 1962. Another strange characteristic of the 5.45am was the fact that it was a stopping train down the Hastings line but had only two intermediate stops between Hastings and Ashford. *David Clark*

Sussex has been well served by third rail electric traction since the 1930s but there was an obscure system that used the overhead supply principle. This was the Hellingly Hospital Railway which was authorised in 1899, at an estimated cost of £2,000, and ran for about a mile between Hellingly station, on the 'Cuckoo Line', and the East Sussex Lunatic Asylum, as it was known at the time. The line was initially used to convey building materials and stores, a contractor's steam locomotive being used on this chore. In 1902 it was decided to electrify the line at 500 volts and an electric passenger car was used to convey patients, staff and visitors to the hospital which formally opened in July 1903. There was also regular goods traffic in the form of coal, for the hospital's central heating boiler, and provisions, and these goods trains were operated by a diminutive steeple cab electric locomotive, the precise origin of which is unclear. The locomotive is thought to have been of German origin – the control equipment appeared to be German – and the names of two British firms appeared on maker's plates but neither firm had any record of its manufacture. This contraption was reportedly limited to two loaded 12-ton coal wagons up the steep gradient to the hospital. This fascinating little system closed to passengers in 1931, but remained in use for goods workings until 1959 when the hospital's boiler was converted to burn fuel oil. The last loaded coal wagon was taken up to the hospital on 10th March 1959 and this was returned to Hellingly station on 25th March. This illustration shows the tiny electric locomotive, coupled to a BR goods brake van which tends to emphasise its small proportions, at Hellingly on 4th April 1959 during a visit by the Norbury Transport & Model Railway Club. This was almost certainly the last journey over the line, apart from the occasional jaunt conveying hospital staff only. The photographer comments that the party arrived at Hellingly behind BR Standard Class 4MT 2-6-4T No.80016. *John Langford*

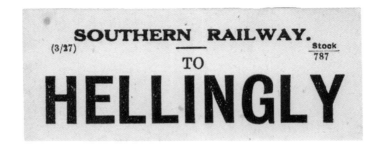

SOUTHERN RAILWAY.
(3/27) Stock 787
TO
HELLINGLY